# HACKING

## INSTRUCTIONAL DESIGN

# HACKING

## INSTRUCTIONAL DESIGN

### 33 Extraordinary Ways to Create a Contemporary Curriculum

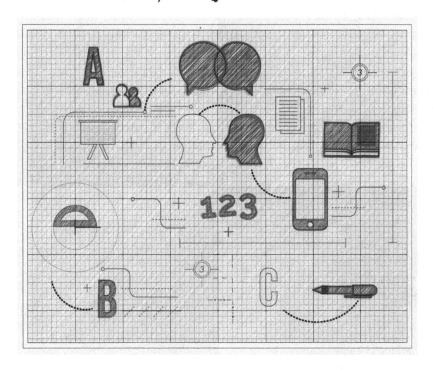

 HACK™
Learning
SERIES

MICHAEL FISHER
ELIZABETH FISHER

*Hacking Instructional Design*
© 2018 by Times 10 Publications

These books are available at special discounts when purchased in quantity for use as premiums, promotions, fundraising, and educational use. For inquiries and details, contact us at www.hacklearning.org.

Published by Times 10
Highland Heights, OH
Times10Books.com

Cover Design by Najdan Mancic
Interior Design by Steven Plummer
Editing by Carrie White-Parrish
Proofreading by Jennifer Jas

Library of Congress Cataloging-in-Publication Data is available.
ISBN: 978-1-948212-11-3
First Printing: November, 2018

# TABLE OF CONTENTS

# DEDICATION

To our first teachers, our parents, Douglas and Barbara Brumpton and Michael and Terry Fisher. What we learned about being good people and good parents we have learned from you. We love you and thank you.

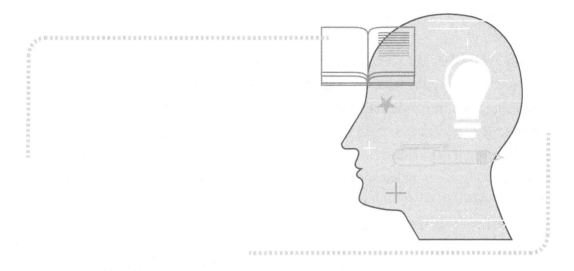

# PREFACE
## Be loyal to learning and learners

IN 1892, THE National Education Association convened a group of educators that included the commissioner of education, heads of several colleges, and principals of notable high schools. This group, called the Committee of Ten, was tasked with reimagining the structure of the American high school curriculum. Their recommendations included the standardization of what schools offered, the fact that students would go to school for twelve years—eight in elementary and four in high school—and the promotion of equity in instruction regardless of a student's path after school was over. Sound familiar?

Now, 126 years later—*126 years!*—we are still struggling with how we do school. We still organize most of our high schools in this structure from 1892. Many of our students must still meet seat-time requirements to get a diploma rather than demonstrate what they actually learn. Adhering to this structure has created massive problems with equity across our country and limited our students so much that many need remedial help in college before they are ready to meet the demands of higher education. In terms of careers, the private sector is spending $3.1 billion a year to bolster entry-level workers' literacy skills.

Both H.G. Wells (in 1920) and Janet Jackson (in 1989) have shared that we are in a race between education and catastrophe. Sixty-nine years apart and we're still struggling with the same sentiment—and that's almost thirty years since Jackson included the declaration as an interlude on an album. We must be mindful that the education we provide doesn't lead to catastrophe. As such, we want this preface to be a mobilization for our profession, a preparation for a revolution, a manifesto of sorts to energize and invigorate all educators.

Our primary, contemporary, essential question is this: How do we truly prepare our learners for their futures?

The way we've always done it has run its course. When we think about how we are going to prepare our children for life after school, nostalgia is no longer on the table. We need to focus on the things that matter to the student, the student's world, and how the world will receive this student into its global citizenry.

So, what is it that matters to contemporary students and their learning? For one thing, we must own the fact that we are in charge of all the structures that make up our system of schooling: the schedule, the time, the place, what is offered, how it is offered, how we assess (locally), and how we build interdependence. We must have critical conversations about all these things, as well as what we value about learning. Do we want students to learn or not? Or rather, are we more concerned with physical attendance, seat time, check-off lists of tasks, grades that represent desired behaviors rather than learning, and busywork?

If learning is our goal, then there are ideas that we, as educators, need to consider about our contemporary students:

- **We must understand that our students are not naive.** They have voices, and we need to recognize that their voices are paramount to their learning. As they get older, student voices lead to learning choices, and it becomes extraordinarily important that we invite them into mature and increasingly sophisticated conversations about how the system is supporting them and their learning. We want them to shift their thinking from authoritarian receivers and "us versus them" mindsets and make them true collaborators in the learning that matters to them.

- **We must be transparent in practice.** If we're going to help students see possibilities within the challenges, we need to be as transparent as possible around access to information, learning resources, and options that launch learning rather than limit it. That means we must be open to communication and collaborations both as leaders and learners, and boldly hack away at any hidden agendas or curricula. Everything out in the open. All the "what ifs." None of the "maybes," "next times," or "buts."

- **We must turn passion into action.** In a March 2018 CNN report, a six-year-old named Naomi from Bend, Oregon, found a fossil in the dirt adjacent to the soccer field her sister was playing in. Naomi knew the rock she found was special, and as news of her find spread, she was connected to the director of Paleontological Collections at the University of Oregon's Museum of Natural and Cultural History. While the sixty-five-million-year-old fossil was not scientifically significant, it started an arc of inquiry that may well be the entry point into a career that Naomi had never considered, insofar as six-year-olds are debating career paths. We are seeing what differences students can make when they turn the things they care about into actions that demonstrate their learning and show the world, not just their teachers, what extraordinary things they can do.

  Think of Alexandra Scott, the young lady diagnosed with neuroblastoma at the age of four, who created Alex's Lemonade Stand and raised over one million dollars for children with cancer. Think of Anne Frank, the most well-known documentarian of World War II. Think of Louis Braille, who, at three years old, was blinded by an eye injury. While studying at the Royal Institution for Blind Youth in Paris, Louis invented a system of reading for blind people based on raised dots, known today as Braille. Think of Claudette Colvin, a fifteen-year-old student from Booker T. Washington High School in Montgomery, Alabama. Arrested for the same offense as Rosa Parks—not giving up her bus seat—Claudette's challenge toward civil rights laws eventually led to a Supreme Court order that outlawed segregated buses. Think of Malala Yousafzai, the Pakistani student who was inspired by her father's humanitarian efforts and rose to prominence by writing blogs about her life living under the Taliban occupation. A Taliban gunman shot her in retaliation for her activism. She survived and went on to become the youngest Nobel Prize winner ever. She continues to be an advocate for education and human rights.

Students are thirsty for investigating what matters to them. We must give them that chance. Our current system of education shouldn't be the barrier that hinders their learning; it should be the fuel that launches it.

- **We must defend innovation.** We need more innovation in schools. We're getting nowhere with antiquated curricula that blocks creative problem-solving and cross-disciplinary learning. Students need to learn things that are just in time rather than just in case. In order to innovate, students need to take risks, make mistakes, and fail. And then do it again. And then do it again. Failing early and failing often creates a cycle of iteration and a learning mode that invites trial and error, discovery and exploration, and intrinsic motivation.

- **We must identify bright spots.** We need to look for successes so that we can replicate them. This is a central tenet in Dan and Chip Heath's book *Switch*. To maintain motivation, we must celebrate what works. Those bright spots become launching pads and can bring together collaborators who want to share in future successes. Students need to know that they are making a difference, and ultimately that they can replicate their successes—and those bright spots—in multiple ways by applying what they've learned and celebrated.

- **We must create a culture of connection rather than a culture of correction.** How we interact with each other matters now more than ever. We are the only humans in the history of humanity who have been as well-connected as we are now. That's a lot of overlapping of talents, and a lot of opportunities. Yet we are losing the possibilities that lie within the overlap by continuing to separate politically, socially, and culturally. Communicating and collaborating are key 21st-century skills. We need to practice them, model them, advocate for them, and teach our students how to do them well. That includes inviting students into their own learning in ways we've never done before, honoring their voices, and co-creating choices for learning and assessment.

- **We must eliminate the culture of threat.** We must push aside the negative aspects of schooling that linger from decades of authoritarianism. When we think about something as simple as grading practices, we are horrified by the fact that, even in 2018, grades continue to represent both achievement and behaviors rather than being simple indicators of learning. Students, particularly public-school students, are bound by social mores that sought to attune students to a life of committed acquiescence rather than creative trailblazing. Educational programs that continue to include suspensions and expulsions, punishments and negativity, need to be re-evaluated. Programs like Restorative Justice and Invitational Learning are paramount to erasing the influence of authoritarian structures and "the way we've always done it" mentalities.

- **We must commit to our objective of loyalty to learning and the learner.** It no longer matters just what students know. It matters what they can do with what they know. Contemporary students don't necessarily need teachers to gift them with knowledge. Knowledge lives everywhere now. Everybody has access to everything. Contemporary students *do* need teachers to help them sort, sift, connect, sophisticate, construct, create, explain, and evaluate all that is out in the ether.

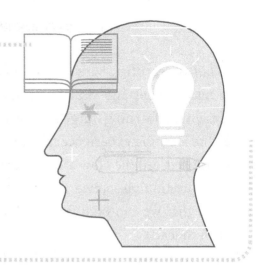

# REFOCUS YOUR EFFORTS ON WHAT REALLY MATTERS

INSTRUCTIONAL DESIGN IS an important function in the role of teacher. It is not a product for teachers to receive; it is a crucial, creative responsibility of the job. That which teachers design, detail by detail, is the foundation for their other roles: guide, docent, disseminator, explorer-leader, coach, cheerleader, assessor, instructor, and director. The students will also build their learning on this foundation, as they become more than just receivers of information, but grow into explorers, performers, product managers, discoverers, champions, masters, players, evaluators, and ultimately, creators of anything imaginable.

A teacher's curriculum is a compendium of documented decisions and it includes many facets. As such, all the internal elements of a curriculum should be symbionts in an academic ecosystem, each with its own niche, function, and form. Having well-designed elements of that ecosystem is integral to student success and performance. This includes imaginative and innovative experiences that strengthen the ecosystem and keep it vibrant and growing.

First, we must understand what makes up a curriculum. A curriculum details the *What* of learning, based on standards and how we break down those standards into content and skills, essential questions, big ideas, transfer goals, and the design of learning targets. The documentation of the curriculum details *When* the learning experience falls in the academic calendar. The documentation instructions detail the *How* and include methodologies, resources, student contributions, questioning, networking, and projects. Then we use a variety of assessments so that we can qualify *How Well* the students learned what we intended for them to learn.

In this book, we're going to tackle all of those: the *What*, the *When*, the *How*, and the *How Well*. We're also going to discuss the *Why*, in terms of how we contextualize the learning for the learner, and we will also broach the topic of *Where* the learning will happen. We've laid this out as a menu—a set of options—rather than a linear list of must-dos, and as such, readers should take care not to read this book as a sequential list of steps to contemporary curriculum nirvana. Such a thing does not exist. Rather, we hope that you will read this through a lens of personal relevance and resonance. Note that in this *Hack Learning* book, we deviate from the formulaic structure of the other books in that there are no sections called A Blueprint for Full Implementation or Overcoming Pushback. All the Hacks in this book are potential blueprint items, and our main pushback is on creating collaborative cultures that promote consensus and collegiality, which we address repeatedly. Look for what speaks to you and act on it accordingly. That's the umbrella Hack here: Get what you need, with a nutshell explanation, and come back to the book when you're ready for more.

There is a level of duality to the Hack nature of this text. Besides giving you "just in time" access to what you need when you need it, these Hacks are also meant to simplify complex processes. This book is meant to make instructional design easier and provide you with thinking topics that should fit with other types of curriculum models you have experienced or are currently working with. These ideas represent a compilation of experiences rather than being tightly aligned with one way to do this or another. One of the big takeaways here is that you can create instructional design in countless ways and it can still be valid, reliable, and contemporary.

The point is for you to be the designer, not the recipient, of a curriculum. Your professional practices are much more effective when you explicitly know standards, curricular elements, assessments, and contemporary instructional practices. And then, you put that professional knowledge to work, collaboratively with colleagues, to craft an instructional program based on the designed curriculum that meets the learning and engagement needs of every child.

If you are like many teachers or curriculum specialists, you will start with your own compilation of experiences, and in that case, use this menu of Hacks to target where you want to grow. This mode of design is intentionally programmatically agnostic. If you already have plans, maps, and units, choose whichever of these Hacks resonates with you in terms of places you can reflect or improve upon. If you're designing a new unit or thinking about instructional design in general, it is perfectly appropriate to skip around and choose what you want to use, though you may want to give priority to the Foundational Hacktions.

Students are at the heart of all our instructional decisions. They are the reason we do what we do. We want to provide students with school experiences that give them both roots and wings. We lay the foundation, then let them fly. We want to do the same for you, the reader, with our menu of instructional design considerations. We wish roots and wings for you as well.

Now, let's get to work *Hacking Instructional Design*!

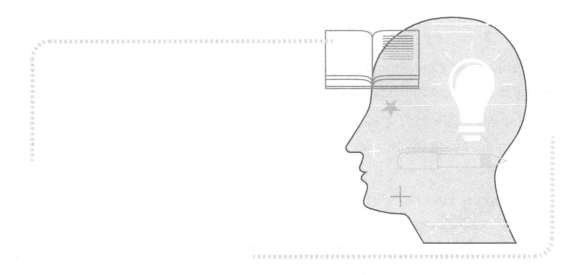

# HACKTIONS

## Hack*tion

/hakSH(ə)n/

*noun*

A category or group of Hacks that are organized according to a particular hacky topic.

Hacktions represent a range of Hacks that seek to uncomplicate a previously complicated thing or act.

This book includes categories of Hacks that we are calling *Hacktions*, each of which serves a separate function for either instructional design or contemporary instructional planning. While there are many ways for teachers to teach and students to learn, we prioritized this set of Hacktions based on our experiences with thousands of teachers and their instructional design needs.

Foundational Hacktions. These Hacks are related to the foundations of the curriculum, including breaking standards down into their component parts, aligning practices with standards, and figuring out how to turn standards into learning goals and targets. These Hacks are what teachers engage in before the students arrive in their classrooms.

Instructional Hacktions. These Hacks look at instructional elements, including prior knowledge, vendor products, multiple modalities, inquiry design, assessment, and lesson experiences. The Instructional Hacktions, along with the

Engagement and Contemporary Hacktions, are what teachers (and students!) will engage in when the students are in the classrooms.

Engagement Hacktions. Beyond the Instructional Hacktions, these Hacks explore opportunities for creativity, wonder, motivation, and engagement for the deepest of learning.

Contemporary Hacktions. These Hacks delve into what is currently on the horizon in terms of educational opportunities that modern students care about. It gives teachers a chance to explore new opportunities that were never possible before.

Blueprint Hacktions. These Hacks look at how educators will draft and document their professional plans. Each one offers multiple ways to think about laying out plans, appraising them, and developing new cultures around curriculum and assessment.

# FOUNDATIONAL
## HACKTIONS

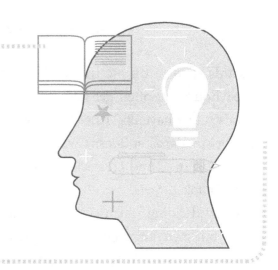

# HACK 1

# GET R.E.A.L.!

## Make the standards work for you and your students

### THE PROBLEM: TOO MANY STANDARDS ARE OVERWHELMING FOR TEACHERS

THE BREADTH OF standards is overwhelming for teachers. Many feel like they are barely scratching the surface of learning and are instead simply following prescribed curricula with fidelity to standardized tests. This leaves many teachers asking how they can make sound and unique instructional decisions while still aligning to the standards.

### THE HACK: GET R.E.A.L.!

To make a difference in student learning, teachers need to understand that some standards have priority over others. Standards purists might say that each standard is necessary and important, but the reality is that narrow bands of standards are assessed, and some have a high degree of overlap. Teachers need to decide which standards are important, and how they match with their own plans.

When working with curriculum design in any form and trying to decide how standards need to dictate that design, the best approach is to take it one step at a time. Educators often get bogged down with the big picture, particularly when administrators have an "I need this done yesterday" mindset. Though that might work for standards, it doesn't work for everyday curriculum. Journeys such as this are taken in steps and are easiest when teachers set goals according to manageable and attainable targets.

Start by deciding which standards should take priority, and how those standards fit into your own curriculum design goals. This helps to deepen learning, strengthen curriculum design efforts, and create better learning experiences for students. Once you determine what your priorities are, you can align your curriculum to those priorities. Additionally, work with your department-level team or grade-level team so that you're all teaching the same standards during given instructional periods. This will give your students a guaranteed and viable curriculum, regardless of the teacher. We subject too many students to an "educational lottery," where they have teachers who don't collaborate, converse, or come to consensus about standards—and that decreases the students' abilities to learn.

To determine whether a standard needs to be a priority in the first place, get R.E.A.L. This stands for Readiness, Endurance, Assessment, and Leverage. Use the following guidelines to break down standards into levels of importance and priority as you design your own curriculum.

### R: Readiness

If a learning moment is dependent on a previous learning moment, then it is imperative that students be prepared for that. Each step must prepare them for the next so that we don't drag them into learning they aren't yet ready for. Skipping steps builds gaps over time and creates lifelong anti-learners who aren't willing to try. We certainly don't want that! Be sure that students are ready by engaging some of the suggestions in the upcoming Hacks, specifically the Hack on prior knowledge. Focus on readiness before you move on to the next standard, to make sure you're giving your students the best possible chance at advancement.

### E: Endurance

Any concept or idea students learn that will serve them from now on is considered a lifelong skill, like understanding text structures or automatically knowing multiplication tables. Fluency in sight words and easy math facts should be automatic for students so that they can move on to more challenging problems and texts. If they don't understand the basics, they are going to struggle with anything that comes next.

Skipping this concept, though, occurs when teachers try to cover their standards more quickly due to time or administrative constraints. When that happens, students don't nail down the foundational elements of a specific content area. Without those enduring, lifelong skills, students will struggle to move to the next step of learning, which will lead to ever-increasing gaps in proficiency as students get older. As teachers, we must understand what these enduring, lifelong skills are, as informed by the standards, but also by our professional knowledge as effective educators—and focus on them before moving forward.

## A: Assessment

The "A" in R.E.A.L. doesn't just stand for Assessment. It stands for *Any Assessment at Any Time*—a variation of an idea first written about by Fenwick English. The idea here is that students should be as ready for an assessment as they are to receive new learning; as opposed to assessing students only when they are prepared, such as at the end of a unit or the end of a week. Making sure students are ready for assessment at any time means teaching the standards in a logical way that builds upon previous knowledge and gives you a guideline for curriculum design and priorities. Consider including formative and/or benchmark assessments as dress rehearsals for their final or summative assessment performances.

For readers who are concerned about standardized assessments, note that state education departments often publish testing guides well before state assessments occur. These testing guides specifically tell educators what standards will be assessed, though they don't often say how a particular standard will be represented. If you don't know about testing guides or assessment overviews for your state, ask your administrator or search your state's education website for key terms such as *testing manual, testing guide, assessment guide, assessment overview, or test or assessment framework.*

## L: Leverage

Another angle for determining standards priorities has to do with leverage and which standards will have a high degree of overlap in other classes/content areas. For instance, if students are learning about ratios in math, what are the chances that they will also be learning about them in health, physical education, the sciences, or career and tech ed classes? Students learn better if all their teachers work together on overlapping ideas like this, and cooperate in their teaching methods. Doing so requires the teachers to know their standards and work in tandem in terms of schedules, as well as prioritizing these areas of overlap.

# WHAT YOU CAN DO TOMORROW

- **Think in bundles.** Know which standards go together both thematically and conceptually. In the math standards, conceptual groupings are usually built-in. In literacy standards, you must have an awareness of analogues and relationships. For instance, when students are asked about evidence in text, you might find that evidence to have descriptors in multiple standards. These standards might also be related to writing standards, where students are asked to write using evidence in text. There may also be natural relationships to speaking and listening standards, as well as language standards. Consider bundled standards instead of individual standards, to teach with more precision and allow your learners to learn more deeply.

- **Begin reorganizing and reimagining your current curriculum to reflect priority standards.** Based on what we know about standardized assessments around the country, priority skills such as analytical reading, foundational math concepts (readiness/fluency), and scaffolds for sophisticated demonstrations of learning are assessment anchors on these tests. Make sure to represent these standards-based skills regularly in your curriculum.

- **Make sure you represent your priority standards often in your documented curriculum.** Dig into your design documents and look for redundancy and overlap with whatever you determine to be priority standards. This does not mean that you should engage with these standards in the same way in every class. It *does* mean that you should bring them up with regularity as you design/enhance curricular units over the course of the year. Make sure your level of sophistication throughout a year's worth of learning is steadily moving up. For instance, in the lower-grade-level reading standards, students are asked to describe characters in a story. *Describe* is a lower-level verb. This same standard also asks that students explain how character actions contribute to the sequence of events in a story. *Explain* is a higher-level verb. Although these two verbs live in the same standard, teachers sometimes only teach to the *describe* part, and don't necessarily get to the higher-level thinking of *explain*. What we're challenging teachers to do is understand what's in the priority standards and increase the sophistication of the skills within those standards over the course of the year. You might have Reading Standard 3 in every unit, but after the first unit, you should be looking to increase your students' thinking, growing them well beyond just describing a character and its traits, and moving toward explaining how those traits advance the action by comparing and contrasting those traits among characters in a story. Eventually, students should be able to express themselves in writing and provide evidence for their explanations, comparisons, and contrasts.

Note: *These tips for understanding priorities are a mash-up of the work of several educators: Fenwick English, Heidi Hayes-Jacobs, Janet Hale, Larry Ainsworth, Grant Wiggins, Jay McTighe, and Susan Udelhofen. If you're looking to develop a more structured system around the prioritization of standards, look for publications by these educators.*

## FINAL THOUGHTS

Knowing the heart of the standards and speaking the language of the standards proficiently helps teachers fit them into their own instructional design efficiently and responsibly. For greater student success, make sure you communicate and collaborate with your fellow teachers regarding the standards.

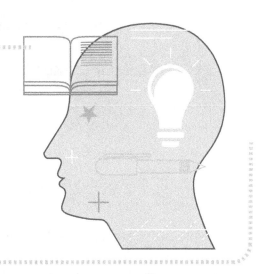

# HACK 2
# GET COZY WITH THE STANDARDS
## Dig in to go deep with the standards' language

### THE PROBLEM: TEACHERS DON'T DEEPLY UNDERSTAND THE LANGUAGE OF THE STANDARDS

**T**EACHERS OFTEN HAVE a clear understanding of what they are supposed to teach, whether it's from an existing curriculum, a vendor product, or years of collected strategies. They don't think they necessarily have to know what's in every one of the standards, nor do they have time to spend getting to know the heart and intention of each one. Then, when there is a glitch in the learning process or students don't perform in the expected way, they often explain it away with student behaviors (like laziness or apathy) but it is rarely based on an understanding of the targeted or intended skill.

### THE HACK: GET COZY WITH THE STANDARDS

Grab a blanket and a mug of hot chocolate and dig into those standards like a five-year-old digs into ice cream. Savor every word and notice the nouns and the verbs. Larry Ainsworth has written about this process for decades, and in simplified form, only asks that the analyzers pay attention to a couple of parts of speech. Let's take this math standard, for example.

From Ohio's Mathematics Model Curriculum for Seventh-Grade Geometry:

*Solve problems involving scale drawings of geometric figures, such as computing actual lengths and areas from a scale drawing and reproducing a scale drawing at a different scale.*

- Note the major nouns: scale drawings, geometric figures, lengths, and areas (the *What*).

- Note the major verbs: solve, compute, and reproduce (the *How*).

The major verbs here will help us build a skill statement. (In subsequent Hacks, we'll detail how to turn these into learning targets and goals.) In this case, we're going to arrange the verbs from lower-level to higher-level and create statements that represent *How* we're going to engage the *What*:

- Lower-level thinking: Reproduce a scale drawing at a different scale.

- Mid-level thinking: Compute actual lengths and areas from a scale drawing.

- Higher-level thinking: Solve problems involving scale drawings of geometric figures.

Note that this standard, while short, contains three discrete skills. This happens a lot in standards. At this point, we have basic skill statements, but they are devoid of how we are going to assess them. Will students use manipulatives for the scaling? Will they recognize proportional relationships from the original figure to the scaled figure? Will students draw or model their scale drawings? Can they explain orally and/or in writing? There are so many ways we can assess these three skills, but we want to be mindful of both the standards' intentions and the time in which we have to work with them, particularly if they are part of a group of related standards, or in this case, related to a specific domain or cluster in mathematics.

If we add language that points us toward how we might assess these skills to the skill statements, it might look something like this:

- Reproduce a scale drawing at a different scale using manipulatives.

- (Associated) Draw and reproduce a scale drawing from a scale chosen by the teacher.

- (Associated) Draw and reproduce a scale drawing from a scale chosen by the student.

- Compute, through drawing and written descriptions, actual lengths and areas from a scale drawing, documenting what the scale is to the original, then calculating the corresponding related length and related area with information from either the original figure or the scaled figure.

- Solve problems involving scale drawings of geometric figures, including written descriptions of the relationship between the original figure and the scaled figure, and reproduction (drawing or model) of a scaled figure with given dimensions of an original figure. Discuss solutions, orally and in writing, using math language.

> AS INSTRUCTIONAL DESIGNERS, WE'RE
> WORKING TOWARD MAKING SOMETHING
> EASIER RATHER THAN MORE ARDUOUS.

This level of standards literacy gives us opportunities to dig into the heart of the standards, right down to the assessment level. In this case, we have translated the standard into something that we can assess.

- Reproduce a scale drawing chosen by the teacher using manipulatives.

- Reproduce a scale drawing chosen by the student (or other students) using manipulatives.

- Compute actual lengths and areas from two figures, one original and one scaled, through drawing and written descriptions.

- Calculate the corresponding related length and related area with the original's given measurements.

- Write descriptions of the relationship between the original and scaled figures.

- Discuss solutions, orally and in writing, using math language.

That's six assessable moments from just one standard statement! That said, the Hack here wouldn't be a Hack if we asked the reader to replicate this process for every single standard. As instructional designers, we're working toward making something easier rather than more arduous. In the real world of teachers with little time, we would note the nouns and verbs for a handful of related standards at once, such as what we described in the previous Hack around bundling standards. From there, we would create our skill statements and layer in assessable actions that make sense in relation to the bundle of standards, rather than just one.

# WHAT YOU CAN DO TOMORROW

- **Notice related verbiage.** When you look at what you already have documented, does the verbiage from the standards flow from standard to content to skills to assessment? Does the assessment measure the standards' intentions? Is there a variety of levels of thinking and cognition in the standards? If so, does that same variety exist in instruction and assessment? Assessing your current curriculum documentation with your colleagues would be helpful here, particularly as answers to some of these questions. If the answers to these questions are not what you want them to be, bouncing ideas off others will help you improve your curriculum. Discuss ways in which you can realign your documentation, rooted in the collegial understanding of the intentions of the standard.

- **Practice unpacking standards alone, and then with colleagues.**
  Based on the quick example in this Hack, practice unpacking some of
  your standards, and try to understand what each standard is seeking
  from students. Encourage your colleagues to do the same, and then
  come together and compare what you did. Did you all agree on a
  given standard's intention? Did you all pull out the same elements? Did
  you have similar ideas about assessment? Compare your answers and
  use your colleagues' answers to strengthen your own.

- **Defer to the expertise of you and your colleagues.** If you
  come across a standard that is vague or has limited information, use
  your best judgment about unpacking it and how you will assess it. In
  the New York State Next Generation Learning Standards for Third-
  Grade Literacy, students are asked to *conduct research to answer questions, including self-generated questions, and to build knowledge.* This is
  broad, and we can interpret it in multiple ways. The major verbs are
  *conduct, answer,* and *build.* The nouns are not specific and are therefore
  open to many different interpretations. Some questions that might arise
  include: How do students conduct the research? What questions will
  we answer? How do students generate questions? What knowledge is
  important to build? Does this standard apply to one learning moment
  or multiple learning moments? How will students demonstrate the outcomes of their research? We could go on and on.

  It matters more that you and your colleagues interpret this standard
  in a similar manner so you have equity in practice. It doesn't matter if
  you interpret it differently than we did. We don't know your students
  like you do, and we don't work in your building. Trust each other's
  expertise and work together to figure things out. If you still find yourself
  looking for clarification, use Twitter, Facebook, or Instagram to reach
  out to your virtual networks and engage in online conversations with
  your connections. More insights might live online, as well!

- **Reach consensus on the terms in the standards.** Collegial consensus and teacher expertise are important when unpacking a standard, particularly when that standard is ambiguous or broad in scale. Do all the teachers in your grade level, department, or even school agree on what the *central idea* is? Students deserve teachers who agree on their basic understandings of the standards. We are doing students a disservice if a teacher teaches something in one class and another teacher teaches something contradictory in the next class. Reaching consensus means that each of you can live with it and guarantees consistency for students. Discussions of this sort also help teachers come to a deeper understanding of the standards themselves.

## FINAL THOUGHTS

To translate standards into actionable, instructional practice and assessable moments, break down each standard into its component pieces. From there, you can build your instruction and assessments with intention, and hopefully collaboration, to create the best learning experiences for your students.

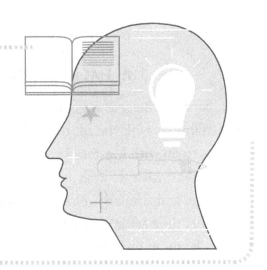

# LEARN TO "BLOOM" AGAIN!
## Achieve cognitive alignment

### THE PROBLEM: COGNITIVE MISMATCH

WHEN CREATING CURRICULA, we spend much time on delineating a standard's intentions and breaking it down into actionable skills, targets, and instructional activities, but sometimes we overlook the cognitive alignment. When we work with teachers on ways to document their curriculum, we often ask how students are performing, so that we can go back into their curriculum and see what sorts of alignment exist already. In many cases, we find thoughtful intention around the *What* but not necessarily the *How*, and, by extension, the *How Well*. For instance, if a standard asks that a student describe and explain a concept or an event in a story, teachers must understand that there are two different levels of thinking going on: describing and explaining. If the documented curriculum or a teacher's instructional decision has students focus more on the description and less on the explanation, but the assessment addresses the explanation only, then there is a cognitive mismatch between the instruction and the assessment. This cognitive mismatch is just as significant as if we assessed students on something we never taught them.

## THE HACK: LEARN TO "BLOOM" AGAIN!

Think back to college and get reacquainted with Mr. Benjamin Bloom. While you may be familiar with the oft-used Bloom's Taxonomy pyramid, his main claim to fame has to do with Mastery Learning. We already wrote about how *readiness* is a lens through which we look at the learner's ability to receive new information and knowledge, and similarly, Bloom proposed that for students to deeply understand something, they actually need to achieve a level of *mastery* before moving on to the next learning moment.

This is antithetical to many current educational practices where "one and done" lessons or assessments are the norm. Mastery Learning takes time—time that some teachers don't feel they have. That said, it's worth thinking about the variety of experiences that students have in a teacher's classroom, and how often the experiences invite students to think at multiple cognitive levels. This is especially important if a standard dictates the level of thinking the students should be doing. However, even if a standard doesn't directly state that multiple levels of thinking are necessary for proficiency, it stands to reason that the deeper we can get students to think about their learning, the better they'll perform on any demonstration of learning.

The Bloom's Taxonomy pyramid isn't a recipe for marching students through increasingly rigorous skill development. It's a reminder that we must create the conditions for multiple experiences with knowledge that supports deep, mastery-level learning. So when a standard says that students should *describe and explain*, perhaps we should also think about having them evaluate each other's explanations. Through their descriptions and explanations, we can more fully explore different ways to apply what they are learning. And, of course, how often can we create something unique as a result of all the learning and thinking we've done together? That is the pinnacle. That is the goal zone.

The main thing to remember is that there should be a variety of thinking going on in the classroom. Varied experiences at multiple cognitive levels are essential for meaning-making, transfer, and student learning and performance. Note that Bloom's pyramid is heaviest at the bottom. You can't jump to higher levels without building the foundation, just like you can't build a house without laying the foundation first. The knowledge is the root of everything, and what "blooms" from that is everything a student can *do* with the knowledge. Remember, too, that the application of the taxonomy is not linear. We might think of the taxonomy as a bush rather than a pyramid. The roots are the knowledge base and the other levels, and all their associated lingo, make up a many-branched bush.

## WHAT YOU CAN DO TOMORROW

So how do you invite those multiple cognitive experiences into your classroom?

- **Analyze your instruction and assessments.** Analyze the alignment of the thinking required during instruction, compared to the thinking required in the assessment.
    - Are the verbs of the standards congruent to the verbs that happen during instruction and assessment?
    - Does the assessed cognitive level of skill match the instruction?
    - If the instruction covered all the content and skills but was on the lower level of thinking, what must be done to increase the thinking level during instruction, to help students do better on the assessment?
    - If there isn't a cognitive alignment between the instruction and assessment, what are you going to do about it?
    - What opportunities do students have to demonstrate their learning in a variety of ways?
    - How are students exploring and discovering and asking their own questions to help steer them toward mastery?
    - What is the same from day to day in your classroom, and how might you shake things up to provide multiple types of experiences that engage multiple levels of cognition?
- **Plan beyond the standard's verbs.** The verbs of Bloom's pyramid are not equal, even when they appear on the same level. They

represent different facets of thoughtful actions. At the *analyze* level, verbs like *explain*, *differentiate*, and *categorize* are just some of the associated words. We think we can all agree that *explain*, *differentiate*, and *categorize* are not synonyms for *analyze*. If a standard is situated at a particular cognitive level, it is up to the teacher (and maybe the students too!) to explore a variety of thinking amongst and across each of the taxonomic levels. When you've broken down your standards into actionable skill statements, take the verbs you distilled from the standards and think of how you could extend the learning using verbs from the same thinking level. Then look to extensions of the skills amongst the verbs in another thinking level, particularly a level that is higher than what the standard intended.

## FINAL THOUGHTS

It is important to use Bloom's as a reference point for discussing the balance of thinking between instruction and assessment. There have been iterations of Bloom's in the ether of educational practice for years, with revisions and spawns of other types of thinking models and progressions toward Mastery Learning. The big point here is to engage students in multiple levels of cognition for the sake of helping them continue to become great and independent thinkers.

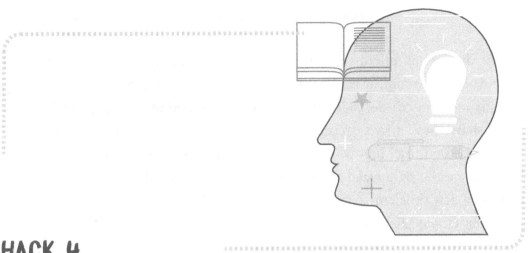

# RIGHT-SIZING THE WORK
## Navigate right-sized steps for students

### THE PROBLEM: LEARNING TARGETS ARE NOT JUST "I CAN" STATEMENTS

L EARNING TARGETS ARE not new in education, but over the years, the understanding of what they are has become diluted and/or misinterpreted to the point that they are misused. Learning targets are not about placing the words "I can" or "Students will be able to" at the beginning of a standard statement. They are also not the same thing as having objectives or a list of skills that students must master. In curriculum work with multiple schools, we often see learning targets that represent more of an objective statement or an overarching learning goal, which we'll discuss separately in another Hack. Objectives and learning goals are too broad to negotiate granular decisions and choices by students and teachers.

### THE HACK: RIGHT-SIZING THE WORK

Teachers want their students to be successful, right? Students want to know that they are progressing toward their learning goals, right? Learning targets, in their correct form, help students see incremental progress toward their goals, like parts of a whole. Think of an apple pie. Each ingredient is a necessary part of the process. The oven is integral. The pie dish is important. The ingredients, the oven, and the dish are all micro-decisions to make when baking a pie. If we apply that logic to the classroom, it leads us to one important question: How can we help students make micro-decisions that feed a larger learning arc? And further, how do we share these micro-decisions with the students, and make sure that we're both focused on reaching the target in a lesson or series of lessons? These micro-decisions are the right-sized steps to reaching a goal, whether it's baking a pie or learning a new problem-solving strategy. Let's look at an example.

In First-Grade Life Science in the Next Generation Science Standards, one of the performance expectations is: *Use materials to design a solution to a human problem by mimicking how plants and/or animals use their external parts to help them survive, grow, and meet their needs.*

When designing the learning target's right-sized steps, we need to pull out the important information here. For this example, students need to understand animal and plant structures and the functions of those structures, how plants and animals keep themselves alive and how their traits contribute to their survival, and finally, how humans can take advantage of those traits for their own survival and having their needs met. All these important pieces of information are learning goals, though, not targets. They are the results we hope to obtain from the project. For the targets—the right-sized, student-friendly versions—we need to go a little more granular. For example:

Learning Goal One:

- Students need to understand animal and plant structures and the functions of those structures.

Right-sized steps for this learning goal:

- Students brainstorm the structures of plants and animals.
- Students speculate on what the structure is used for, or what it helps a plant or animal to do.

Potential learning targets (in student-friendly language):

- I can describe the parts of a plant or animal and explain what each part can do.

**Learning Goal Two:**

- Students need to understand how plants and animals keep themselves alive and how their traits contribute to their survival.

Right-sized steps for this learning goal:

- Students speculate on how a structure, behavior, or trait helps a plant or animal survive.
- Students speculate on how several structures, behaviors, or traits work together to help a plant or animal survive.

Potential learning targets (in student-friendly language):

- I can explain how a plant or animal uses its different parts to help it stay alive.

Note that this is a higher level of sophistication than describing different parts and explaining what each part can do. This is where students start to put together a deeper explanation of integrated structures and how they factor into keeping a plant or animal alive.

**Learning Goal Three:**

- Students need to understand how humans can take advantage of these traits for their own survival and having their needs met.

Right-sized steps for this learning goal:

- Students need to understand the function of structures, behaviors, and traits, and speculate on how humans might be able to use something similar.
- Students need to practice examples orally and in writing regarding how different structures, behaviors, and traits could be used to help humans survive and live.

> GET TO KNOW THE HEART OF THE STANDARD AND WHAT IT IS ASKING OF STUDENTS. BREAK IT DOWN INTO LEARNING GOALS THAT YOU CAN FURTHER REFINE INTO INDIVIDUAL TARGETS.

Potential learning targets (in student-friendly language):

- I can explain the connection between a moth's camouflage and camouflage clothing for humans.

- I can explain how a turtle's shell is like the protective armor a knight might wear.

- I can explain how flippers on my feet help me swim better in the water.

Now that you've identified the learning targets, your students are ready to meet the challenge of the Next Generation Science Standards Performance Expectation of designing a solution to a human problem by mimicking how plants and animals use their external parts to help them survive. The learning targets allow for strategic and specific right-sized learning steps to build the conceptual knowledge that students need for performing the design task.

## WHAT YOU CAN DO TOMORROW

- **Resist the temptation to just write "I can" in front of a standard.** Get to know the heart of the standard and what it is asking of students. Break it down into learning goals that you can further refine into individual targets. Create the learning target(s) in student-friendly language based on the right-sized step(s). We used "I can" statements but it is certainly appropriate to use "We can" or

"Students will be able to" or something along those lines. The point here is to provide access by the students. This target is for them; don't make it overly complicated, wordy, or long.

- **Think of your ingredients.** When you are considering standards, learning goals, or unit objectives, try to get into the habit of automatically thinking of smaller steps or individual actions in the process. Ask yourself questions like, *What do the students need to know before we embark on the next learning moment? Are my formative assessments and pieces of feedback offering opportunities for right-sizing a student's next learning action?* and *What are the individual pieces of content, individual skills, and associated processes that may need explicit instruction?*

- **Invite students to help you.** Even young students can participate in the design of learning targets. The process doesn't have to be as structured as what we are describing here and can be as simple as relaying your overall objectives and asking students how they might meet each objective. Students may have insights that you didn't think of, or they may offer information that serves as a pre-assessment of their starting places around the current unit of study.

- **Collaborate.** Collaborate with your colleagues and collaborate with the students. Take a partnership approach to designing learning targets. It helps if all stakeholders have the same understanding of the trajectory of the learning in your classroom. This is particularly important if you are one of a group of teachers who teaches similar topics or grade levels. Collaborating and coming to consensus about the meaning of the standard and the learning targets you tease out of it means establishing and maintaining equity for all students. Additionally, when teachers collaborate well, they are modeling collaborative cultures for their students.

## FINAL THOUGHTS

It is helpful to right-size learning targets for students, particularly if they have a hand in what those right-sized steps will be. Learning targets help students achieve at a deeper level, which, in turn, helps them perform better.

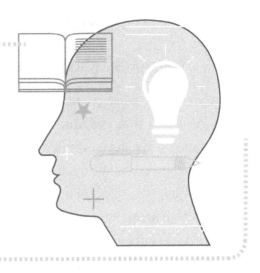

# MAXIMIZE LEARNING BY SETTING GOALS

## Help students navigate their own learning

### THE PROBLEM: EMPHASIZING DOING OVER LEARNING

"GIVE ME THE basics and I'll do something extraordinary," said no student ever. More than likely, a student will say something along the lines of, "Just tell me what I have to do."

Conceptual-level deep learning is often (but not always!) overlooked in favor of covering a curriculum in a way that suggests it is a timed race rather than an opportunity for students to deeply explore a new topic or learning experience. This deep-learning version of teaching asks students to be self-directed and motivated about their learning, which is difficult when they are doing surface-level tasks, which are not technically learning. Even worse, many of those tasks don't have any meaning or context for the student and are likely forgotten as soon as the test is over. There's a big difference between doing something and learning something, and to truly learn deeply, students must set their sights on destinations and then work to get there.

## THE HACK: MAXIMIZE LEARNING BY SETTING GOALS

When we think back to elementary school, we remember a lot of wishin' and hopin'. Wishing that assignments wouldn't be too difficult and hoping we'd get a good grade on whatever we had to do. The learning was there, but it wasn't necessarily the purpose. We'd learn or do whatever the teacher asked us to do, and if we did it well, we got good grades, and everybody was happy.

This new generation of learners is different. The wishin' and hopin' days are over. They meet learning goals when we specifically plan for them and map out pathways to achieve them. This includes reflective analysis about the steps in our plan and how we are progressing toward a goal. But these actions are not just for teachers. In *The Quest for Learning*, co-authors Marie Alcock, Michael Fisher, and Allison Zmuda wrote about several ways to help students learn to set goals. One of those ways is right-sizing instructional steps based on learning targets, which we covered in the previous Hack.

When we move from teacher decisions to student decisions, we invite motivation, buy-in, and high performance because we have intentionally included student voices and ideas into the planning. What we're really doing when we help students set goals is helping them self-regulate their work, persist in reaching their goals, and become more metacognitive about their decisions and thinking. There are multiple ways to do this. Here are four:

1. **Learning targets:** We can give students the learning targets we've distilled and ask them to come up with further action steps to reach each target. (Note that you can also invite students into the creation of the learning targets!) See Image 5.1.

| Learning Target: | Action Steps: |
|---|---|
| Learning Target: | Action Steps: |

Image 5.1: Learning Targets

2. **KPL chart:** We can give them habits in the form of a riff off the KWL chart (what a student Knows, Wants to know, and has Learned). In this case, we call the chart a KPL and ask students to document what they **Know**, what they need to **Practice**, and what they still need to **Learn**. As an additional idea, our colleague Silvia Rosenthal Tolisano (langwitches.org) adds an additional "H" to her KWL chart, and we think it is appropriate to add it to ours as well. The H stands for **How** the student is going to learn. See Image 5.2.

| KNOW: | PRACTICE: | LEARN: | HOW: |
|---|---|---|---|
|  |  |  |  |

Image 5.2: KPL Chart

3. **Navigation checkpoints:** Speaking of the *How*, students can also plan how they might demonstrate that they've learned something by choosing how they will be assessed or what they might create as a result of learning. Then, the goal-setting becomes a navigation of checkpoints as they proceed to their goal (the deliverable). These checkpoints can be mini-due dates for completion of tasks, right-sized action steps leading up to the checkpoint, or

group responsibilities and task management for group members if the deliverable is collaborative. Note: This could easily shift into a checkoff sheet that would undermine the learning and focus more on the doing. Coach students through the documentation of their learning or make sure that the majority of what they document is leading to the learning goal/deliverable. See Image 5.3.

| Deliverable / Assessment / Project / Challenge | Learning Checkpoints: |
| | Timeline Checkpoints: |
| | Group Responsibilities: |
| | Completion Deadline: |

Image 5.3: Navigation Checkpoints

4. **Shaded targets:** We've also seen teachers use a list of learning targets for students to color or shade as they become proficient with the target. It's a quick visual check for both students and teachers to see how students are progressing toward their goals. You could extend this by having students highlight in yellow. Teachers can highlight in blue if they agree on the target and/or notes, and students can then see in green what proficiencies they are earning. See Image 5.4.

| Learning Targets: | Anecdotal Feedback / Notes: |
|---|---|
|  |  |
|  |  |
|  |  |
|  |  |

Image 5.4: Shaded Targets

# WHAT YOU CAN DO TOMORROW

- **Invite students to the goal-setting table.** Students need planning documents, too. While educators might understand the need for curriculum documentation in whatever form it is in, students are rarely involved in the conversation. In college, professors often give students a syllabus or a calendar of upcoming events, but that doesn't happen in K–12 schools. Yet even in a collegiate effort, students aren't invited to the planning table. Professors just deliver the curriculum and the goals to them. Use the planning ideas above to solicit student input. You can give them to students collectively as a pre-planning organizational tool when a unit begins, or use them singularly when the moment arises.

- **Shift accountability and be ready for wobbly beginnings.** Put students in the driver's seat regarding decisions about how they will learn and how they will demonstrate their learning. Be ready for silence at the beginning. When ideas do start flowing, you may need to push a little to get to a contemporary action or assessment. Embrace the "what-if" zone of this type of curriculum navigation. Be

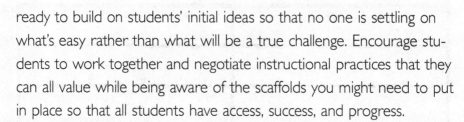

ready to build on students' initial ideas so that no one is settling on what's easy rather than what will be a true challenge. Encourage students to work together and negotiate instructional practices that they can all value while being aware of the scaffolds you might need to put in place so that all students have access, success, and progress.

- **Make the ideas your own.** After using a couple of these documentation ideas, start remixing, revising, and recreating your own organizational tools. The examples above are meant to demonstrate ways in which students can organize and document their thinking, not be the *only* ways they can contribute. In fact, once you've successfully co-navigated through this with students, or shown them a variety of ways, let them choose how they want to document their goals and action plans by either selecting one of the methods you taught them or creating one of their own. When you or your students create new ways of doing this, we encourage you to share online using either @fisher1000 or @elizabethfisher, or the hashtag #HackLearning.

- **You don't have to jump into the deep end.** We know that what we are asking is a big deal. We're asking trained experts and professionals to relinquish control of some aspects of the learning process to those who have little training. But inviting learners into the process gives them a voice that promotes buy-in and motivation. It's OK to wade into the pool here and give students deeper and deeper water as time goes by. Inviting students, even with baby steps at the beginning, reclassifies them and their roles in the classroom. They become valued voices—and they become more committed to their own learning.

## FINAL THOUGHTS

While we are primarily suggesting here that teachers encourage students to co-create decisions in the classroom, we also recognize that not every class or teacher is ready for that. Even a slow relinquishment of control shifts responsibilities to students, and that creates better opportunities for ownership and deep learning.

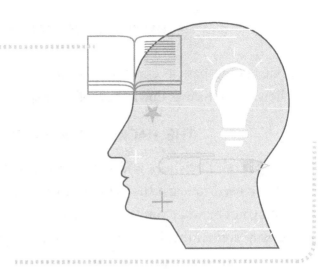

# HACK 6
# GET BEHIND THE WHEEL
## Don't be a backseat driver

### THE PROBLEM: TESTS AND ASSESSMENTS AREN'T THE SAME

**T**EACHERS OFTEN LUMP together tests and assessments as a catchall term for how students will demonstrate their learning. Even with all that is known about testing and assessments, teachers often find it difficult to break out of their habits and instead promote opportunities for students to show what they know in an isolated test event. Bad testing habits that we've learned include giving tests because we're at the end of a chapter, the end of a unit, or because it's Friday. Even worse is giving the test and then marching forward into a new unit or chapter without addressing learning improvement areas or giving the students any meaningful feedback.

Teachers must get back into the driver's seat and take control of their vehicles if they want students to make positive gains, and if they want to understand what students know. Just giving tests (particularly when using vendor products), aligning with traditional practices around testing, or using years-old lesson plans is like being a backseat driver. You're letting someone else or some tired tradition be in charge of running your classroom. You can talk about how you might do this or that, but talking has no effect whatsoever on the way the car is driven, where it goes, how often it slows down, how often it speeds up, or where it eventually stops.

## THE HACK: GET BEHIND THE WHEEL

Buckle up, grab the wheel, and step on the gas. It's time for a little intentionality.

First, we need to learn the primary differences between tests and assessments. A test may not be what you think it is. Tests outside of education measure quality, or the way something is performed, or perhaps a medical number of significance. Tests in school are what we would consider checkups for retention, but that blanket term is only rarely intended as a barometer of deep understanding. Think spelling tests, pop quizzes, and chapter tests. Tests, in their current form in many places, allow for the regurgitation of knowledge in a particular moment but do not necessarily tell the evaluator much about the learner.

Assessment is the word you're looking for and the word you should get into the habit of using—if you don't already.

> THE GOAL OF ASSESSMENT IS NOT SIMPLY TO MEASURE ACHIEVEMENT, BUT TO UNDERSTAND WHAT A STUDENT HAS LEARNED AND IN WHAT WAYS THEY ARE ABLE TO USE THEIR KNOWLEDGE.

Assessment connotes evaluation, and in an educational context, an assessment is meant to evaluate students' learning and what they can do with the knowledge. Grant Wiggins and Jay McTighe refer to this as *transfer*, where students are not learning tidbits of information for the sake of a test, but are truly understanding, so much so that they can perform under a unique set of circumstances.

There are multiple types of assessment. Diagnostic assessments measure an individual student's skills, strengths, and weaknesses. Formative assessments include ways for teachers to capture evidence of student learning while the students are still learning. These are also known as assessments *for* learning. Summative assessments are assessments *of* learning and represent more of an end point where students can demonstrate their collective understandings. There are other types of assessments, such as projects, problems to solve, and more contemporary ways to assess, that we will review in other Hacks. Here, though, we want to underscore that *quality* is more important than *quantity*, and that the goal of assessment is not simply to measure achievement, but to understand what students have learned and in what ways they are able to use their knowledge. Real assessment is the heart and soul of the meaning of *How Well* that we described in the introduction.

How students use and apply their learning is essential. In their work around *Understanding by Design*, Wiggins and McTighe often say that what students know is not nearly as important as how they use what they know. There's a great scene in the fifth Harry Potter book, *Harry Potter and the Order of the Phoenix*, where the new Ministry-appointed Defense Against the Dark Arts teacher Dolores Umbridge is explaining to students that they will be learning about defensive spells in a risk-free, theoretical way. They won't *use* the magic, they'll just *read* about it. This is the first class in five years where students are learning a theoretical basis for spells but will not, in fact, get to try them out. When the teacher reasons that this is a risk-free way to learn, the students counter with the fact that if they are attacked, it will not be risk-free. Ultimately, the students create their own class to practice defensive spells so that they know what to do in the moment they need to do it. They practice, critique each other's performances, and hone their skills under variable conditions.

While we'd love to see this level of student contribution to instruction and assessment in the classroom, we wouldn't want it to happen in *spite* of the teacher's actions, but as an invited action. So how do we start focusing on assessment—and inviting the students to add their voices to the instruction?

# WHAT YOU CAN DO TOMORROW

- **Assess your assessments.** Assessments can be multifaceted and do not necessarily have to occur over one class period or even on one particular day. Use a variety of assessment types to paint the best picture of learning. Good assessment involves actions, such as constructed responses, building models, explanations, and evaluations—something beyond remembering and recognition so that the student can answer a bunch of multiple-choice questions. Take an inventory of the assessments you currently give to students. Do they measure what is easy to measure or do they measure what matters? Do they have depth and substance or are they more drill and skill? How can you reimagine your assessments to provide you with a more detailed understanding of what students have learned? How can your assessments be more contemporary? How can you co-create your assessments with students?

- **Let the students drive sometimes, too.** Invite them into the conversation by asking how they would like to represent what they've learned. What are some different ways they can demonstrate their learning? There are several Hacks in this book that seek student input, including the Hacks on goal-setting and getting personal. We've woven in ideas about students as contributors throughout this book because it matters very much that students chip in with their own ideas around how they will demonstrate their learning and show what they know.

- **Shift the audience.** When assessing your assessments, ask, "Who else are my students accountable to?" Audiences matter for contemporary learning experiences. The current generation of students is highly concerned with who sees their work and the many places they can share it. Part of a teacher's responsibility is, therefore, to help students solicit feedback about their learning from someone besides the teacher. This can be student-to-student in the classroom, or outside the classroom via a publishing platform like YouTube. It could be the publication of their work on a variety of websites that have commenting features for the world at large. (Teachers would need to monitor comments, teach students how to give quality comments and not just praise, and be ready to jump in as needed if public comments go awry and need mediating.) The feedback the students get from whatever audience they engage should go into the revision and edits they make to their work before submission or publication. Note that the audiences here could still include the teacher; we're just advocating for the audience to be not *only* the teacher.

- **Shift your mindset.** Do you want to collect a bunch of grades or do you want to know how your students are progressing toward their learning goals? We understand the reality of the culture of schools. We were in classrooms ourselves where we had to generate grades. While we're pleased that some places have shifted to documenting proficiency with standards or individual learning goals, that isn't happening everywhere yet. Report cards and grading systems haven't changed all that much in the last few decades, and we need to rethink what we value in the system. The goal is learning. It's transfer. It's the ability to apply the learning to a variety of unique circumstances. That starts with the teachers, so begin building a list of things you'd like to do or see in your classrooms with this shift in mind. If you'd like to learn more about shifting to a new mindset, check out Starr Sackstein's Hack Learning book *Hacking Assessment: 10 Ways to Go Gradeless in a Traditional Grades School.* You can also join the Facebook group: Teachers Throwing Out Grades.

## FINAL THOUGHTS

Assessment should do two things: provide information about students' progressions toward their learning goals, and qualify (not quantify) *How Well* they've met those learning goals. Assessments are not for generating grades. They are not for generating data sets used for any purposes other than improving the learning of those whose data was collected. They are not meant to be used for teacher evaluation or efficacy (particularly as one yearly measurement as a blanket for quantifying a year's worth of learning or value-added measure). Assessments and tests are not the same thing, and it's time we start differentiating between them in our instructional design, for the benefit and empowered learning of our students.

# INSTRUCTIONAL
## HACKTIONS

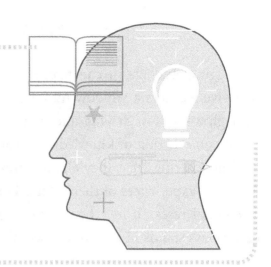

# PLUG INTO PRIOR KNOWLEDGE

## Anchor new learning

### THE PROBLEM: PRIOR KNOWLEDGE IS NOT ALWAYS ENGAGED

O NE OF OUR largest educational conundrums is deciding what, how, and why students need to learn, and making sure we're moving in a logical direction as we guide them. We can utilize the greatest resources in the world, but unless we're connecting to previous learning or experiences, we're not taking advantage of the neural pathways in a student's mind. Prior knowledge exists outside of standards, outside of grade-level expectations, outside of assessments, and outside of the numerous pedagogical ideas we're sharing in this book—but it is a vital piece of any student's education. If we want learning to stick, we need to anchor it in a way that allows students to build on their existing foundations, using their prior knowledge.

### THE HACK: PLUG INTO PRIOR KNOWLEDGE

Students grow neural pathways when new learning builds on knowledge that already exists in their brains. Plug students into their own brains to figure out where to start. You don't put a roof on a house with no walls or foundation, right? You lay the foundation first; the same theory is true in the classroom.

Plugging students in can happen in multiple ways: through pre-assessments that give teachers a window into existing knowledge, or through discussion, or through a series of driving questions. Students can also participate through the social construction of knowledge. Social construction has to do with a group of students sharing what they already know, which allows students to build on the ideas and experiences of their peers. This instills background knowledge without traditional research in a book or dictionary—and gives you an idea where the entire class stands in regard to a starting point.

## WHAT YOU CAN DO TOMORROW

- **Ask and answer questions.** One of the biggest missing features in many classrooms is rich discussion. We often ask students to approach new learning by reading about it rather than discussing it. Read a chapter, answer the questions, take a test on Friday. Sound familiar? If we want students to demonstrate what they've learned, though, we need to lead them down a trail that allows that. Discussion means listening and speaking, and can lead to reading, researching, reviewing, and reflecting on what everyone said. After that, they can write, perform, or problem-solve with unique parameters. In this way, you're setting out a common level of prior knowledge with the discussion, and then allowing students to build on that individually and demonstrate their knowledge. See more about questioning practices in the Hack on inquiry.

- **Teach students to notice and think.** On Harvard's Project Zero website, you can access several types of Visible Thinking routines that we've used with students and teachers over the years. They are spectacular for teasing out details in conversations and inviting rich discussion. One that we use often is "See, Think, Wonder." Over the years, we've changed it slightly to Notice and Think. When we invite learners to use Notice and Think, we're looking for them to notice what jumps out at them as important—specifically, information they think is worth knowing and sharing. Then we ask them to make connections between that and anything else that they've read or experienced. Using this thinking routine has led to many deep conversations over the years, and we still use it when working with teachers today.

• **Activate the students' mental Velcro.** In the book *Active Literacy Across the Curriculum* by Heidi Hayes Jacobs, we were introduced to the term "mental Velcro." She describes how we want the learning to stick... like Velcro. This idea, along with many others in brain-based research, talks about the emotional attachment students must have to their learning in order for that learning to stick. This happens in several ways. First, students must connect new learning to previous learning for this to work. Second, students need opportunities to experience different forms of instruction. If everything is always the same from one day to another, it keeps them from taking the next step and figuring out which way works best for them. It certainly keeps them from achieving a deeper level of learning. Third, students must get excited about their learning. When they do, they are more motivated, they retain more, and they remember for longer periods of time. Look for ways you can change your curriculum to account for these requirements so you can activate emotional hooks within your students and engage that mental Velcro. Switch up your methodologies, add humor to the learning, add color, engage their interests, and provide multiple types of media.

• **Time travel to 1949.** Take a quick trip back in time to 1949 to Ralph Tyler's book *Basic Principles of Curriculum and Instruction*. He outlined the foundation for what you hold in your hands right now, and the foundation upon which we seek to build as you read and contemplate instructional and professional goals. It's important to set clear goals and objectives, create lesson experiences, and evaluate how students are progressing toward their goals; then make decisions about how you will measure your and your students' successes in meeting those goals. It is equally important to remember that new learning is dependent on connections to previous learning, and that teachers must understand what their students are bringing to the table with them. That includes any innovations and right-now experiences that students may have already become accustomed to in their current generational realities, even if those innovations and experiences differ from their teachers' experiences.

## FINAL THOUGHTS

Activating prior knowledge is essential for helping students make connections. Those connections provide the basis for students to build on as they grasp new concepts and ideas. Devoting time to prior knowledge as a function of new knowledge acquisition is an essential component of instructional design.

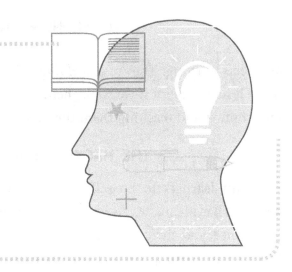

# HACK 8
# PUT IT INTO CONTEXT
## Help students understand the why

### THE PROBLEM: STUDENTS DON'T UNDERSTAND WHY THEY'RE LEARNING WHAT THEY'RE LEARNING

WHENEVER WE WALK into classrooms to work with teachers and students, we take every opportunity to ask students to tell us about what they are doing and learning. When we ask what they are *doing*, they can almost always tell us.

- "We're studying for our upcoming test."
- "We're reading in our books."
- "We're following these directions to do our science experiment."
- "We're making a PowerPoint about ancient civilizations."

When we ask what they are *learning*, however, they often have no idea, or are less sure. When we ask why they are learning what they're learning, we get crickets.

The problem is, students aren't connected to what they are doing or learning if they don't know *why* they are doing it. In that situation, they're not accomplishing any deep learning. They're just *doing*. We have to make the learning matter and make it have a point if we want them to retain anything. We do that by putting it into context and teaching them the *Why*.

## THE HACK: PUT IT INTO CONTEXT

We want learners to be self-directed, interested, and free of stigmas around failure. That means we need to think of interest, motivation, engagement, curiosity, voice, and choice. Those who have used Montessori approaches or Universal Design for Learning models will recognize some of these elements. To succeed, we must make sure that students are squarely rooted in the *Why* around their learning. The context matters as much as the content, perhaps even more, as it helps students learn more deeply and build on dispositions like initiative and persistence. If they understand *Why* they're doing something, they'll work actively until they've mastered the learning.

Let's take our bullet point above about ancient civilizations learning and play it out a bit. Suppose the teacher asks students to read about the Incas, the Mayans, and the Aztecs. As a demonstration of comprehension, let's say the teacher also asks them to create a slide presentation that includes pictures and text to describe the contributions of each civilization. The teacher has chosen the text, the task, and the mode of the demonstration. Students read the text, perform the task, and use PowerPoint to display their work. How does the teacher know that the students learned anything? The students have completed the task list. Check off, check off, check off, done.

Now, let's add the context angle. We still have a root in ancient civilizations. The associated standard here is: *Students compare and contrast the geographic, political, economic, religious, and social structures of the Incas, Aztecs, and Mayans.* Maintain the reading and research but include a variety of texts and associated media for students to choose from. Maintain the need for a deliverable, but don't require PowerPoint for all. Give students choices and voices for how they will demonstrate their learning (voices meaning valued) and let them contribute ideas that the teacher will consider.

The teacher, along with the students, will navigate choices for the students around each of the structures listed in the standards, such as geographic, political, and economic. Each group now investigates the Incas, Aztecs, and Mayans with a contextual frame, which is two-fold in this case because of the standard (using geographic structures in this example):

- Investigate geographic structures of the Incas, Aztecs, and Mayans.

- Compare and contrast geographic structures among the three civilizations.

- What were their contributions to modern civilizations?

The last bullet point, while not a solid, essential question, is a probing question that provides an additional contextual frame. Students choose to learn about a particular structure, but they are also learning about the contributions that ancient civilizations made to modern civilizations. This is beyond the standard, certainly, but adds a little more depth to the *Why* of what the students are investigating.

> LISTENING TO STUDENTS' VOICES ABOUT HOW THEY MIGHT DEMONSTRATE THEIR LEARNING CREATES NEW OPPORTUNITIES FOR BUY-IN, INTEREST, AND MOTIVATION.

Inviting their voices for the assessment/demonstration of learning might yield a variety of products, including:

- A website that documents the similarities and differences between these three ancient civilizations.

- A podcast where students moderate a Q&A around multiple structures that were influential in the creation and maintenance of these civilizations.

- A movie (animated or filmed) that shows the impact of these structures on ancient civilizations.

- A Minecraft creation, complete with script and voice-over, that shows representations of these civilizations and their contributions to modern civilizations.

Listening to students' voices about how they might demonstrate their learning (which we will discuss further in the Getting Personal Hack) creates new opportunities for buy-in, interest, and motivation. This gives students context for understanding exactly *Why* they are learning what they are learning. When we focus on context over content and ask students *Why* they are learning about ancient civilizations, their answers will sound more like:

- We're trying to find out how the geography of the land helped nomadic people begin to settle down, and how they shaped the land for their needs.

- We're researching societies among the Incas, Aztecs, and Mayans to find out how each civilization established law and order.

- We're using Minecraft to reimagine an Aztec temple and the water surrounding it to illustrate how people who lived in Tenochtitlan used the water to build giant chinampas, or floating gardens, for growing food. We're going to build something similar for the Incas and the Mayans once we find out what they did for food and how they used the land.

# WHAT YOU CAN DO TOMORROW

- **Invite the kids into the design conversation.** It's OK to relinquish control around some of the choices for learning and demonstrating learning in the classroom. As the teacher, you are responsible for the *What*, but the *How*, the *Why*, and the *How Well* can be co-navigated. We've said this a couple of times already, but it applies here as well.

    - Ask students *How* they like to learn new things.

    - Ask them *How* they might show what they know.

    - Listen to their ideas and try to either incorporate them verbatim or help the students shape the ideas, so they feel that they have some control over how they will learn and be assessed.

    - Allow yourself to play with time. Fixed content plus fixed times for learning do not equal fixed learning. In their book, *Pyramid Response to Intervention,* authors Austin Buffum, Mike Mattos, and Chris Weber posit that in order to "fix" the learning (fix meaning secure), teachers must vary the content and the time for learning it.

    Doing these things creates buy-in and motivation for learning that might not have been there before. Also, let the space for these conversations be safe places to sandbox ideas and try them out before committing. Put all the clay on the table and help them shape it.

- **Constantly and respectfully ask them *Why* they are learning whatever you task them with learning.** Ask them why they are exploring or researching in a particular way. Ask them why they are making the choices they make. Ask them to reflect on why they made a decision. Ask them why what they are doing right now matters to their end goals.

- **Encourage them to explain their *Whys* to each other and to anyone else they encounter.** Students gain much learning through their explanations. Encourage students to explain their choices, their findings, and their progress toward their goals to anyone who will listen. That includes other students and the teacher, and audiences beyond the classroom walls. Additionally, they can share any of the potential co-created assessment choices online, ideally in a place that offers feedback or commenting.

## FINAL THOUGHTS

Students always want to know why they are learning this or that. Giving them the context or situating their perspectives promotes self-direction, motivation, and deeper learning.

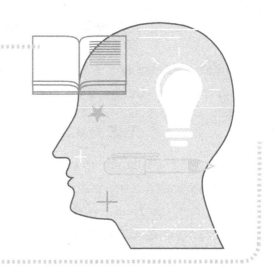

# BALANCE THE CONTENT

## Realize that thinking is important, but we have to have something to think about

### THE PROBLEM: JUMPING TO RIGOR AND EXPECTING BETTER TEST SCORES DOESN'T WORK

IT'S SUCH A modern problem to have.

New standards in language arts, mathematics, social studies, and science, and in standards beyond the four core courses, are all emphasizing a singular common idea: Students need to learn how to think. We agree. We've spent the better part of the last two decades teaching students *What* to think, knowing all along it wasn't a great practice, and ignoring the idea of teaching them how to think for themselves. The focal points should be on the *How* and the *Why*. No brainer, right? But in the wake of new standards, there's been a push in the rigor to make everything analytical and dig into the *Why* before the *What* has had a chance to dry.

To be good thinkers, students need to know what it is they're thinking about. What problems are there to solve, and what resources do they need to know to solve those problems? Content, like the prior knowledge in a previous Hack, is a foundational element to learning, thinking, and performing. We cannot just jump to the rigor and hope for better test scores.

## THE HACK: BALANCE THE CONTENT

Students need a balance of content-building and critical thinking. Building on prior knowledge is important since that gives new content a foundation upon which to rest, but that content knowledge can't stand alone. It must include the thinking that goes along with new learning and the acquisition of new ideas.

Discipline-specific expertise comes from being introduced to new ideas and concepts through exploration, discovery, inquiry, networking, play, and/or game design. (We will discuss each of these later in the book.) Students need time to delve in, to find *Aha!* moments, ask questions, find resources (both physical and digital), and have sandbox time to play with new ideas without fear of failure.

To maintain the balance of building new knowledge and thinking critically and creatively about it, we must give students multiple opportunities to share what they are learning through speaking and writing. The speaking part is especially important. We often visit classrooms and discover that students are struggling with written responses to a question or scenario. When we talk to teachers about the learning process, we might find that they deleted or never planned for the storytelling and conversational or oral explanation pieces. Thinking through a response, a solution, or a creative remix of ideas requires that students talk. This is their sandbox, where they can try things out and see what works and what doesn't. It is a collaborative and communicative space where students can share their ideas and benefit from the ideas of others before taking the cognitive leap to expression through writing. This is of particular import for students who struggle with the written word, and who are working through multiple ideas and concepts concurrently. If they're going to demonstrate their learning, they need a safe space in which to sound that learning out. They need both content learning and time for critical thinking. That balance is absolutely imperative for the learning to stick.

# WHAT **YOU** CAN DO TOMORROW

- **Talk time.** It is critical for students to be able to talk, discuss, tell stories, and orally describe and explain, and do so in pairs and small groups. While it is a cognitive stepping stone to higher-level expressions in writing, oral expression involves a handful of soft skills students also need: being able to communicate with others, listening and speaking in turn, and learning to have shared conversations where there is a balance in speakers and ideas shared, rather than one or two students dominating. Start planning for places where you can give students talk time, so they can learn how to work their ideas out via speech and brainstorming.

- **Shared writing.** Before you ask your students to attempt written responses on their own, plan opportunities for shared writing in pairs or small groups. Apps like Google Docs can help you accomplish this, but you don't necessarily need technology to make it happen. One of the cool features of Google Docs is that students can chat within the document before committing ideas to the main page. This continues the idea of a sandbox where they can play with ideas before putting them down in the more formal area. From our experience, as writers, there is no better teacher than collaboratively writing something with someone else. Ideas get bigger and bolder and the products have bigger WOW factors!

- **Do real research.** Get rid of the way you've always done it. If you already know the outcomes of a research opportunity—or worse, if the students already know the outcomes—then it's not real research. It's just a collection of facts that are already known. As an example, on the way in to work this morning, white stuff was falling from the sky. We were hesitant to say it was snow, as we could hear it hitting the windshield. It wasn't exactly sleet either, as the noise it made wasn't as clinky as ice pellets. Once we parked our car and got out to investigate, we observed that it was white, but not crystalline like a snowflake. This was an in-between hybrid thing that was neither a snowflake nor a sleet pellet. Other observations included the fact that the temperature was hovering around the freezing mark, and that during the previous day and up until that morning, we had high winds, decreasing temperatures, and off and on rain and snow. What could these white frozen things be? And how did they form? Answers to these questions can launch a phenomenon-based exploration and discovery opportunity that allows students to build on their background knowledge, gain new knowledge, and think critically about the conditions necessary for this hybrid frozen mystery. Further, we can make this a teachable moment or extend it into something we're already doing in the curriculum around content: learning about the weather, or writing an informational piece about what we researched and discovered. Invite real research into your curriculum design to create real lesson experiences and achieve real learning.

- **Don't remove students for any reason during new learning time.** We know scheduling is hard, but if students are going to be building strong content knowledge, they can't do so as a makeup or rush job. When students are pulled out of the classroom, make sure it happens during practice time rather than during introductions of new ideas and concepts. Pulling them out during new learning time doubles the load on students who often struggle with the regular load. The adults in the building need to make critical decisions about scheduling that support students in the best ways possible, rather than scheduling that helps them in one area but is a detriment to learning in another. Scheduling should not be about adult convenience. Instead, it should be about balancing all learning equally.

## FINAL THOUGHTS

Content, or the *What* we referred to in the introduction, is a major part of instructional design. Without it, we're left with skill development with no real purpose. We can't just gift students with the content in hopes that they will receive it, remember it, and perform it. They must have multiple explorations with many driving questions in order to own the learning.

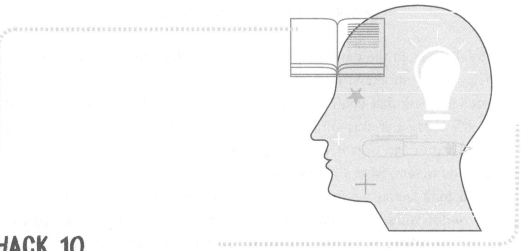

# CREATE LESSON EXPERIENCES AND ABANDON GRANULAR PLANS

## Understand why granular daily plans aren't as effective as they used to be

### THE PROBLEM: GRANULAR LESSON PLANS LIMIT REAL LEARNING

**B**ECAUSE OF MANDATES, systemic adherence to tradition, or just for lack of another way to look at instructional design, lesson plans remain stalwarts in classroom instructional practice. Teachers spend hours creating something that is only marginally useful for most, and that tends to encapsulate learning rather than setting it free. Lesson planning does allow teachers to *cover* all the nooks and crannies of the curriculum… but largely prohibits them from helping students *uncover* the learning. In short, this method limits real learning. (See the Hacks on Curriculum (In)Fidelity and UN-cover the Curriculum.)

### THE HACK: CREATE LESSON EXPERIENCES AND ABANDON GRANULAR PLANS

What do you remember about school? The worksheets? The spelling tests? The reading and answering questions? Do you have better recollections of activities that stood out from the day-to-day march through the curriculum? Things like field trips? Guest speakers? Performances?

There's a reason that you remember more details about field trips than worksheets. It's because it was different. Your brain remembers differences better than similarities and organizes your experiences according to how emotionally engaged you were in what you were doing.

In 1916, John Dewey wrote a book called *Democracy and Education: An introduction to the Philosophy of Education*. In it, he writes that "the first approach to any subject in school, if thought is to be aroused and not words acquired, should be as unscholastic as possible." Dewey knew over 100 years ago that in order for learners to truly and deeply learn something, they need to be given something worth learning rather than just something to do.

Forty years later, Ralph Tyler added to this idea, writing that "teachers must have some understanding of the kinds of interests and background to the likelihood that a given situation will bring about a reaction from the student; and furthermore, will bring about the kind of reaction which is essential to the learning desired."

> ### THERE'S A DIFFERENCE BETWEEN THAT WHICH IS TIMELESS AND THAT WHICH IS ANTIQUATED.

Isn't it amazing that facets of contemporary instructional practice were already being researched and implemented that many years ago? Doesn't it make you wonder what happened? How did we get stuck in this racetrack of traditional educational values that promote speeding through a curriculum like a race car driver? Does the speed matter more than the journey?

Thinking of learning in terms of *lesson experiences* rather than tasks or granular plans will help increase student engagement, interest, and performance. Ask yourself the following questions: *How can I reframe the learning so it is an authentic experience, like a field trip or a performance or working toward a contemporary product? How can I co-create learning experiences with students to help them connect their learning to their interests, backgrounds, cultural relevance, or prior knowledge? Build up the context and foundation for the learning to make it an experience, and you will drive students into a deeper and more active understanding of the material.*

# WHAT YOU CAN DO TOMORROW

- **Make bold, contemporary decisions.** There's a difference between that which is timeless and that which is antiquated. You have to throw away the antiquated. Contemporary students don't value it, and the return on investment is minimal. Think big and bold. Think about what you can do now that you could never do before. Invoke the popular phrase, "Go big or go home!" If you take a big risk, there are only two things that can happen: You either soar or you sink. And if you sink, then you learn a way *not* to do that thing when you jump in again. Start by deciding on some antiquated things you can throw away: tests on Friday, spelling lists (especially for middle and high school), canned demonstrations and experiments with known outcomes, rows of desks and authoritarian structures, rote memorization, lectures…. Replace them with experiences like bold projects, contextual vocabulary with socially constructed definitions, real exploration and discovery through observation and co-created experiments, groupings and furniture defined by the task, just-in-time learning, and co-creation and co-teaching, and you'll see a big difference in student excitement and knowledge retention.

- **Wading in is OK, too.** We are absolutely pushing buttons here and hopefully sparking a discussion between you and your colleagues. We were also classroom teachers and are aware of the potential roadblocks to going big or going home. If you need a less frenetic option, it's OK to slow things down so long as you're moving in the right direction. You may want to try sandbox strategies with one class, or even with a small group of students. Try things out a little at a time and build up to the bold. Visit other teachers who already do the things you want to try and get a feel for their organization and processes before you launch your own classroom revolution.

- **Understand that students will have a variety of experiences regardless of the teaching.** Even if you change nothing about your instruction, your students already have differing experiences, depending on their levels of interest and engagement. Where one student learns the bulk of what you expect, another student might only catch bits and pieces, and another absorbs nothing at all. With so much riding on engagement and interest, it stands to reason that switching up strategies and removing the sameness in the curriculum will change the level of attentiveness. Sure, those students may still have varied experiences, but the chances of every student getting at least something out of the lesson are a lot better.

- **Maintain standards and assessments within your new guidelines.** Whatever you decide to do, you should still relate it back to the standards. They are the basis for your instructional actions. It's certainly fine to work above the standards, but don't go so high above them that students struggle. Your decisions should still be rooted in the language of the standards. They're an integral part of the system, just like the assessment, and though you can replace and modernize the assessment, it still has to measure what it is supposed to measure based on the standards.

## FINAL THOUGHTS

While we realize that schools and administrators may still require teachers to turn in granular plans, we hope that this Hack specifically, and the whole book in general, starts conversations around contemporary practices that save teachers time and deepen student learning. We are provoking here, and we're doing it to start conversations about what really matters in instructional design.

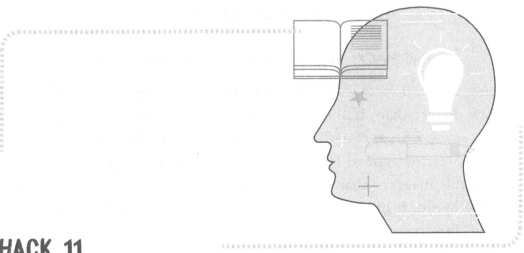

# MULTIMEDIATE THE INSTRUCTION
## Invite multiple types of media into instruction and assessment

### THE PROBLEM: TOO MANY TEACHERS STICK WITH PRINT ONLY

**T**RADITIONAL PRINT LITERACY has been the backbone of learning structures for hundreds of years. Educators pay careful attention to teaching students how to read, and basic literacy skills are the core of early literacy learning. As students get older, we often say that they are shifting from learning to read and heading toward reading to learn. This is quite far from the truth. We never stop learning to read.

As adult readers, we are constantly learning new words and recognizing new patterns and considering the interactions of sounds, images, videos, and text. In the current state of the world, media bombards us from the multiple devices we use, and we're constantly tasked with making meaning that is well beyond just text.

But then we send our children to school, where reading traditional print shouldn't be the only media to which they're exposed. Our current system diminishes other types of media in favor of the tried and true. What's more, when you only deal with print, it means students are only consumers, and never creators. Creating media deepens their engagement and commitment, and thus deepens their learning.

## THE HACK: MULTIMEDIATE THE INSTRUCTION

Bringing in multiple types of media increases the opportunity for critical thinking. Rather than dealing with one media source—text—students get to consider multiple types of media, how they intersect, and how to make meaning from the collected sources. This could be as simple as teaching students how to interact with images or charts embedded within the texts they are reading, and following hypertext links in a digitized text (and coming back to the original text with their new knowledge). Or it could be as complex as accessing media sets that portray different representations of similar or different ideas. If you'd like to see an example of what this looks like on social media, search for the hashtag #pairedtexts, originated by our colleague Jennifer Binis (@jennbinis), where she juxtaposes pieces of media for the sake of dialogue and discourse. That hashtag has caught on with multiple people sharing text, audio, video, and more for the sake of deeper thinking. How might you engage this in the classroom with your students?

What we think about literacy and what it means to be literate have changed. There's a great scene in the movie *Minority Report* when Tom Cruise's character is walking into a shopping mall. When he walks in, a machine scans his eyes, and he is immediately bombarded by voices, still images, pictures, color, sounds, music, and interactive commercials directed only at him and based on everything that is known about him. We think of that scene when we think about how different types of media bombard our students outside of school. The problem is that school doesn't prepare students for dealing with such a scenario. If we aren't preparing our students for dealing with the reality of their future-focused world, we are doing them a disservice.

If we want to prepare our students for that world, students and teachers need to begin considering the following: How much of the media matters? What is the connection between these different types of media? What do I pay attention to and what do I ignore? How can we use this in the classroom?

# WHAT YOU CAN DO TOMORROW

- **Search for associated media.** When reading a text, look for media such as pictures, film bites, podcasts, magazine articles, websites, curated resources like Pinterest or LiveBinders, and museum exhibits that will enhance the thematic or topical issues in the main text. This could be true for class novels as well as textbooks. Multimediating the instruction is an act of creativity in curriculum design, and maximizes opportunities for finding connections, similarities, and differences between the media pieces.

- **Teach students how to look for evidence to analyze their media.** Help students find evidence in the media they analyze by asking them some or all of the following:

  - What do you think the creator of the media wants the audience to understand?

  - Record several details about the media (such as the subject/topic, colors, action, symbols, style, relationships emerging among the different elements in the media, and a comparison to other media).

  - How do the details you recorded support your thinking about the creator's intended message?

  - Repeat the first three with a different piece of media.

  - Go back to the details and look for connections in the media examples. Speculate on why the pieces of media might have been brought together. Give evidence for the connections and ideas that you have.

  - Share your details, inferences, and conclusions with each other, perhaps coming to consensus about meaning, based on what the evidence is telling you.

- **Encourage multimedia products/assessments.** This one is a no-brainer. There are so many tools on the internet today that you would have to try harder to avoid them than you would to include them. Make sure students understand that their ultimate goal is not to use this tool or that, but to meet the objective of the learning through a variety of multimedia elements that showcase literacy on several levels. Our favorite tools include Canva, Sway, Google Slides, Smore, Flipgrid, and Piktochart. You might also guide students to make and share their products online for global feedback. This reminds students that we don't just live in a world of consumption; we live in a world of shared creative experiences.

- **Encourage positive commenting protocols.** As an extension of the previous bullet point, teach students how to add value to someone *else's* work. This doesn't happen when the comments are surface-level compliments or opinionated statements that don't grow the original creator's product. Our colleague Silvia Rosenthal Tolisano has written several blogs on quality commenting practices for students. In those blog posts, she advocates for one or more of the following actions:

    - Students should read a variety of comments on videos, blogs, or other online tools that allow for comments. They should identify comments that are poor, mediocre, or high quality. It's OK for the students to determine their own criteria for what represents quality.

    - Teachers should teach students to avoid surface-level compliments like, "OMG. That was great," "I liked that," or "Way to go." Teachers should also teach students about posting negative comments that don't help the creator grow or revise their work.

    - Teachers should teach students that the comments are meant to extend the conversation and contribute to the impact on learning for all who see the original material and the comments associated with it. If the comment doesn't extend the conversation, or if it elicits a distraction from the main message, it is inappropriate.

- Comments about another's work include asking questions to clarify the message. Encourage students to ask questions about the content they are experiencing to help them situate a perspective or better understand the creator's intentions.

## FINAL THOUGHTS

Our world is demanding that we pay attention to multiple types of media and make genuine connections, evaluations, validations, and choices within those types. We need to start doing the same in the classroom to prepare students for multiple types of media interactions in the real world.

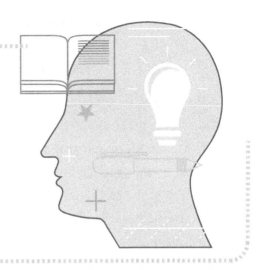

## HACK 12

# INVITE INQUIRY

## Teach students how to ask different types of questions

### THE PROBLEM: TEACHER-DIRECTED QUESTIONING ISN'T INQUIRY

"READ THE CHAPTER and answer the questions." "Your test on Friday will be twenty-five multiple-choice questions." "Make sure all of the questions on the worksheet are completed when you turn in your work."

We've all either done this to students or encountered it in our own learning experiences. Questions are usually directed by the teacher, the text, or gifted to students on a variety of tests/assessments. When the teacher or the text is asking all the questions, then the students are only doing a portion of the learning. If an outsider asks your students what they are learning or why they are learning it, their answers shouldn't be: "We have to fill out the worksheet" or "This was the assignment." As we've discussed before, they need to know the context—and part of that is learning to ask the questions themselves, rather than just answering the teacher's questions.

## THE HACK: INVITE INQUIRY

While this might involve restructuring your instructional practices and require that you relinquish some of the control for who is doing what in your classroom, it's worth the depth of learning involved to invite different types of questions into your instructional practice and put those questions primarily in the hands of the students. Certainly, as the teacher, you are responsible for knowing what content and skills are necessary, which makes you the guide in the learning process. That said, effective guides also leave room for discovery, so those they are guiding have personally enriching experiences.

When students have a voice in how they answer questions and discover new (or refined) ways to investigate, they engage in deeper thinking and produce higher-quality products. But that means they have to ask questions too, not just answer them. Let's look at how this might unfold in a contemporary unit plan:

**The teacher asks a compelling or essential question:**

*"How do musical artists convey meaning and emotion?"*

**The teacher might ask supporting, but associated questions:**

*"How does the way a song is sung impact the meaning of the lyrics?"*
*"How does the way a song is visualized impact the meaning of the lyrics?"*
*"What makes a musical piece/lyrics memorable?"*

Note that the compelling or essential question was a more generalized question, and the supporting questions were more specific.

**Then the students ask their own driving questions:**

*"Do the lyrics connect to the visualization or music video for a song?"*
*"Does the tempo change the way I feel about listening to a song?"*
*"Can certain instruments make me feel different emotions?"*
*"What does the artist mean when he/she writes <insert word or phrase>?"*
*"What do I like about this song?"*
*"What do I not like about this song?"*
*"Why is this song popular or not popular?"*

Note that allowing the students to develop their own questions as a result of the teacher's essential or supporting questions puts students directly in the driver's seat for learning. It also, in a way, helps students delineate learning targets for themselves—bite-sized actionable questions that will give them the knowledge base to more deeply answer the essential questions. See the Hack on Learning Targets for more development of this topic.

**Next, the students and teacher may ask more coaching-type questions of each other, such as:**

*"Does the album this song belongs to give you any other ideas about its meaning?"*

*"As you explore the meaning, how does your meaning change? What changed your mind?"*

*"What else might be important to know about the artist/singer?"*

*"How might the video of the song impact a revised meaning of the lyrics?"*

Obviously, the actual questions here would depend on age and background knowledge, with older students asking increasingly sophisticated and complex questions of each other and the teacher. The point with coaching-type questions is to guide student thinking into an area that they didn't previously consider, or to refine the work they are currently doing.

> MOVE YOUR BODY FROM THE FRONT OF THE ROOM TO THE SIDES AND THE BACK. YOU ARE WORKING *WITH* STUDENTS NOW, NOT *FOR* THEM.

**Students and teachers can also ask reflection-type questions as part of the continued metacognitive growth of the student, or for students to self-assess the quality of their work:**

*"Did I (or did you) do my best during this research project?"*

*"Did you (or did I) find the best evidence to support my question or conclusion?"*

*"What did I learn in this process about myself that might positively impact future work?"*

# WHAT YOU CAN DO TOMORROW

Here are a few ways you can begin engaging in different forms of inquiry:

- **Make sure your essential questions are really essential.** The easiest way is to Google-proof your questions. If you think a question is essential, put the question into Google's search box and press enter. If your search results give you a singular answer, especially if multiple search results corroborate that answer, then your question might not be as essential as it could be. If, however, your search results reveal a variety of answers, particularly with lengthy findings, then your question might be more in the essential realm. The difference between the two types of search results has to do with whether the question is open-ended enough to spark a conversation or debate. If the question has a quick answer, then it's not essential. However, if you ask a question that sparks the next bullet point, then you've likely got yourself a winner!

- **Don't let students answer essential questions... yet!** Change your habits around asking students to answer (with whatever their knowledge base might be) essential or compelling questions. Instead, invite them to ask questions about what they need to research to come up with an answer to an essential or compelling or even supporting question. Then, let their initial questions drive the beginning of the research. Set them free to build background knowledge and *then* come back to the essential question. This lets them become personal contributors to the knowledge-building and gives the teacher an idea of all the facets of exploration that relate back to the essential question.

- **Work from the periphery.** Move your body from the front of the room to the sides and the back. You are working *with* students now, not *for* them. Now you are all sharing questions and research in your classroom, and you will build new questioning habits that take you in and out of different types of questions and who is asking them. You have a niche in your questioning habitat now, and so do your students. For your questioning ecosystem to remain stable, everyone must contribute all the time.

- **Set norms.** It may be helpful to have students create or co-create norms with dispositions, like in Art Costa and Bena Kallick's Habits of Mind, including managing impulsivity, listening with empathy, and thinking interdependently. These could include norms such as refraining from negative body language or not talking over each other during discussions. This will encourage all students to continue with their open question-asking, rather than forcing them to shut down.

- **70/30 split.** Try to start shifting the responsibility for who is asking questions to the students 70 percent of the time. This is not a research-based number, but rather an aspirational goal of sorts. You want students to increasingly ask and answer questions of each other while you step back and let it unfold, unless you need to redirect to address misconceptions, help them refine their explorations, or get them back on track.

- **Invitational question cultures.** When teaching, invite the students into good question-forming habits by flipping the way you engage students in their own questioning behaviors. Often, we ask students something along the lines of, "Does anyone have any questions?" It's a maybe situation at best. If they have questions, great, but if they don't, then the inquiry ends. Instead, try asking, "What questions do you have?" or "What else do you need to know?" or "How can we learn more about this?" These are more definitive. They don't ask for a yes or no, and are instead opportunities for students to create their own driving questions, continue the learning, or contribute their voices about their own needs—all things that keep the learning flowing!

## FINAL THOUGHTS

Questions in the classroom have been a key component of student learning for centuries. In this Hack, we're looking to branch out from tradition and teach students different types of questions and show teachers different ways to coach through questioning. This is the beginning of creating a world of wonder in the classroom, particularly when paired with other Hacks around engagement and contemporary elements.

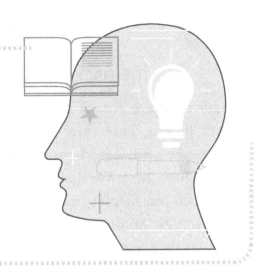

## HACK 13
# ENCOURAGE MORECABULARY
## Create a new culture of vocabulary acquisition

### THE PROBLEM: VOCABULARY INSTRUCTION SHOULDN'T BE ROTE

THE LAST FEW decades have seen much research on word acquisition and process-oriented approaches. That research hasn't led to changes in teaching methods, though. The field is full of respected educational researchers and leaders including Robert Marzano, Marilee Sprenger, Janet Allen, Isabel Beck, Margaret McKeown, Irene Fountas, Gay Su Pinnell, Nonie Lesaux, and many more, all advocating the same thought: Vocabulary acquisition is a process, not a rote task.

Lists of "just in case" vocabulary words and associated busywork activities like writing dictionary definitions and copying the word multiple times do not work. Having a vocabulary test every Friday does not work. We're eighteen years into the 21st century and we're still preparing kids to enhance their vocabulary toolboxes with methods popular in the 1950s. It's time to put this tradition to rest.

## THE HACK: ENCOURAGE MORECABULARY

Pronounce. Engage. Assess.

That's it. Just those three things. Whatever vocabulary you are explicitly teaching, whether it is teacher-selected or student-selected, make sure those three things are happening. Vocabulary instruction in the classroom isn't an event. It's a habit. This is true for all types of vocabulary words, sight words, academic words, domain-specific words, any words! And except for extremely specific, high-level content words, there are no grade boundaries for word acquisition. There may be boundaries for the *assessment* of those words at grade levels, particularly in writing, but for students to own a powerful vocabulary, they must be exposed to lots and lots of words from a very early age in a receptive capacity.

Access equals success, and the earlier the better. Students should have that receptive experience with words early on, even if the expressive level happens later. For instance, it's perfectly acceptable for a four-year-old to use the word "nonconformity" and know what it means, even if the child has yet to understand how letters make words. (Google *Marzano vs. a Four Year Old* if you want to see the video of that.)

Vocabulary practice, at its core, should be a deep learning opportunity. The more we can do to develop high-level vocabulary toolboxes when students are very young, the more we open doors to higher-level texts and media experiences in any content area as they grow older. Effective vocabulary instruction is a gift.

## WHAT YOU CAN DO TOMORROW

- **Stop looking up words in the dictionary.** We should now consider dictionaries, both traditional print behemoths and their digital ilk, as last resorts for discovering meaning. Because of the number of words in our language, dictionary definitions are the shortest and most efficient way to document a word's meaning, likely leaving that definition the least accessible to students when it comes to knowledge transfer. Instead, engage your students when it comes to figuring out the meaning of a word; look for context clues, ask for audience (classroom) intervention, break words apart, explore etymology, think about word families and words that students might already know to bridge understanding, visualize or dramatize the word, and create games with new words. The list of possibilities is infinite.

- **Less is more.** If you want students to deeply learn new words, cut your lists down to a few context-related words that relate to what you're currently teaching. This is a "just in time" scenario rather than a "just in case." Putting students in charge of learning a few words that connect to their current learning will have a bigger payoff than lists of words that are not related. When students learn lists of words out of context or unrelated to their current learning needs, they retain very few of them. It's a poor return on the investment of time and energy.

- **Stop testing vocab lists on Friday.** Friday is not the only day that vocabulary is important, though you'd never guess that was the case in many classrooms today. This practice is still pervasive, and it must stop. Vocab is important every day. We don't want to create neural pathways (myelination) in students' brains that hardwire them to care about vocabulary only on Friday. This level of operant conditioning virtually guarantees that they will forget all they've learned. They cram on Thursday nights to perform well on Friday's quiz or test, and then push it right out of their minds to make room for next week's words. That's not what we want. All words are important. All words need to be in the toolbox. All words need constant (formative) assessment.

- **Be sure to pronounce every new word.** In 2013, we had the great fortune to hear Maya Angelou speak. She was a storyteller, an amazing storyteller, and we sat in rapt attention to her tales. In one of her anecdotes, she told the story of her and her brother Bailey playing Monopoly on her kitchen floor. At the time, she emphasized the first three syllables of "Monopoly," each with a hard "o" sound. She did not learn how to pronounce it until she was eleven or twelve years old and someone told her the correct pronunciation. This made us wonder how often students deal with that same scenario; hence the invitation above for teachers to pronounce every word for their students. This story also reminds me of my roommate in college, who was trying to explain to me that something was understated in an article we were reading for one of our classes. He told me that this something was subtle, and he pronounced the "b" sound in the word "subtle." When I told him the correct pronunciation, he didn't believe me, as he had grown up being told that the "b" was not silent. Imagine that—a whole population of people who mispronounced a word because no one had ever pronounced it for them.

- **Listen for students to use the new words when speaking.** Begin using the vocabulary you want your students to acquire. If you speak it, the students will speak it. Insist that students use the new words when speaking to you or each other. This is part of the constant (formative) assessment I mentioned.

- **Watch for students to use the new words when writing.** When conferencing with them and offering feedback, always question the words they are using and the ones they could be using, particularly the ones that they are currently learning.

- **Engage with words in multiple ways.** Of the researchers we name-dropped in the introduction, every single one of them advocates for students to have engaging experiences with vocabulary that include explaining, examples, elaborations, and extensions. This must be a part of every vocabulary acquisition moment/lesson. Multiple experiences with new words will give them staying power in a student's brain. Students need to be able to first explain new words and meanings orally, and then transfer this to writing. They should be able to provide examples, synonyms, visualizations, and dramatizations of the words they are learning. Students should elaborate on word meanings by making connections to other words, particularly when writing, so they don't develop habits of using the same word over and over. Give students opportunities to extend meanings to other similar words in the same word families, or to interesting words that support the meaning of the original word. For instance, our three-year-old noticed that she could see through both the windows in our house and the windows in our car. We told her (even at three!) that when something is clear like that, it is called *transparent*. Over several days, we played games with environmental examples of things that were transparent: water, air, and some plastic things. We then introduced an extension: the word *opaque*. We said it was an opposite word, and that you *can't* see through opaque things. We played games about what's transparent and opaque enough for us to know that she *owns* these two words. And she didn't have to have a test on Friday to make sure the learning happened!

- **Tell stories about words.** Teachers should share stories about words, particularly when introducing new words to students, and especially when they've got a good story to tell. For instance, when Mike was younger, his parents had a green Datsun B210 with tan, fake leather seats. He lived down south, so the interior of that car was always blazing. He'd get in the back seat and his legs would immediately stick to the "leather," and then the sweating would start and he'd be sliding all over. It was miserable. Add to that an annoying little brother, and there were often arguments in the back of that car. Mike's mother had perfected a reach-around pointer finger that she wagged, while driving, at his brother and him as they continued to argue and misbehave. On one extraordinarily annoying day, Mike thought it would be a good idea to yell at his brother and let him know how insanely stupid he was. Mike erupted, telling his brother at the top of his lungs, that he was *stupendous*. He immediately noticed his mother's pointer finger in action, but the finger didn't complete the action. Instead, his mother stopped short and a smile erupted across her face in the rearview mirror. She said that it was the nicest thing Mike had ever said to his brother. She explained what the word meant, and its meaning is burned into Mike's brain like a cattle brand. Even these many years later, it still stings.

- **Socially construct meaning, both physically and virtually.** Students need opportunities to tell their own stories about words, including sharing experiences they've already had with new words or root words of new words. Teachers, as coaches, should navigate students through their thinking and pull out important facets, helping them to construct, at least at a base level, a workable definition of new words. This can come from context analysis, analysis of root word knowledge, and analysis of prefixes or suffixes. It can also come from their receptive vocabulary—words that live in their speaking/oral language but have not yet made it to their expressive vocabulary, where they know the word well enough to write it or create a demonstration of learning using it. This social construction of meaning is important because it builds on their prior knowledge bases. They already own some of the pieces, and the teacher is helping to build on those foundations and make connections. Teachers can also use virtual tools such as Flipgrid or Padlet, where students can virtually contribute both text and images/videos for the sake of building meaning in expressive ways.

- **Allow students to identify words they want to learn.** New vocabulary acquisition should be contextual and authentic. Besides words that you think are important or that you have identified as potential roadblocks in a text, allow students to contribute words to the vocabulary lists. These words might not be what you intended, but if a student feels the need to go deeper with words they don't know or understand fully, allow them to do so. This enriches their experiences with words and gives them a sense that they are valued and invited to the learning, while encouraging them to be reflective of their work and ask, "Am I understanding what I'm reading or hearing?" If they aren't, they get to make decisions about what would help them understand and comprehend better. This is especially important for students in younger grade levels, special needs students, and English Language Learners. Give all students a chance to highlight words they have trouble understanding and add them to the word work.

## FINAL THOUGHTS

We wholeheartedly believe that stronger vocabulary instruction in a process-oriented approach is the key to maximizing student learning and performance. Over the last few years, we've worked hard to get teachers to see that the way we've always done it isn't working for contemporary students. Vocabulary instruction must be relevant and authentic; just in time versus just in case.

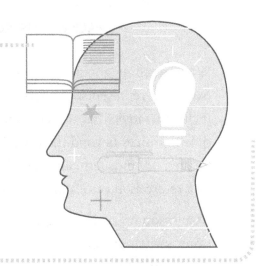

## HACK 14

# PRE-PLAN TEACHABLE MOMENTS

## Make the rare common

### THE PROBLEM: TEACHABLE MOMENTS ARE RARE

THE TEACHABLE MOMENT is every teacher's nirvana. Days are always better when the unexpected or unplanned-for occurrence jumps right into the palms of our hands and the brains of our students. The problem is that those moments are sparse, or only tangentially related to the current learning. But what if they weren't?

### THE HACK: PRE-PLAN TEACHABLE MOMENTS

Those moments of serendipity don't have to be few and far between. In fact, we can absolutely pre-plan opportunities that look a lot like teachable moments and invite students into explorations, discoveries, and higher levels of engagement. We can do this in a couple of ways.

We call the first idea the "Pebble in the Pond." In this approach, we toss a unique situation, enrichment opportunity, or problem into the existing lesson experience. For instance:

- When teaching about the Haudenosaunee Confederacy and the Six Nations it represents, teachers could extend the text-based learning to include a movie that students make about their research, using multiple resources beyond the text. Ask them to make a virtual field trip to a history museum, an invitation to a Tribesman to come and speak, or a re-creation or dramatization of life in the past. (Enrichment.)

- In a lesson on computing unit rates associated with ratios of fractions, switch up the independent practice from the book or worksheet and get the students into Minecraft. Because of its block unit structure, students can model their problems visually instead of with a standard notation. Follow up with a reflective conversation about how visual modeling helps them with the more traditional practice. (Unique Learning Situation.)

- When teaching about circuitry and the flow of electrical energy, start the learning with a circuit problem. Give the students a couple of wires, a battery, and a small light bulb and ask that they figure out how to get the light bulb to light up. (Problem.) While this is a pretty common practice, it is different than reading about circuits in a textbook, because the students are emotionally involved in the actions. Once they complete the circuit, ask them to draw a model of it and describe what they did, then try to explain what happened using as much science terminology as they can. Teachers can use this as both a jumping-off point and a reference point for teaching about circuits.

We call the second idea the "Opportunibox." This approach requires a teacher to have a toolbox of opportunities to pull from when the moment is right.

- **Research quickies.** For this opportunity, students will need an internet-connected device. Allow them to use whatever devices they have to find out more information about a topic in a sixty-second search and be ready to share what they found. Teachers can frame this in multiple ways; for example, as a contest where students must find the most unique information, pushing past anything in the top ten search results, or sharing only one piece of associated media rather than text.

> IN THE MIDDLE OF YOUR EXPLORATIONS OR LESSON ACTIVITIES, STOP THE PRESSES AND ANNOUNCE THAT YOU FEEL LIKE YOU NEED MORE INFORMATION AND THAT YOU ARE GOING TO PHONE A FRIEND WHO MIGHT KNOW MORE ABOUT THIS TOPIC.

- Online formative assessment. Teachers use online formative assessment tools like Socrative, Google Forms, Poll Everywhere, and Kahoot! to quickly gauge student learning. Depending on the results, teachers could reframe/reteach based on an immediately created "Pebble in the Pond" experience or research quickie.

- Nonlinguistic representations or partially linguistic representations. If note-taking is going to occur, challenge students to draw notes rather than writing them just as text. This could be a hybrid model, too, where students both draw and label the drawings as they take their notes. Encourage them to share their notes with each other and revise based on what their peers captured. This is also known as sketchnoting. You can Google the term and see examples or check out a book by our colleagues Janet Hale and Silvia Rosenthal Tolisano entitled *A Guide to Documenting Learning*.

- Phone a friend. Pre-plan a phone call with another teacher, an administrator, an outside expert, or a local community member who can add expertise or thinking points to whatever you are teaching. In the middle of your explorations or lesson activities, stop the presses and announce that you feel like you need more information and that you are going to phone a friend who might know more about this topic. Call the friend or expert and put them on speaker. This is especially effective if students can ask the expert questions. Taking it a step beyond, ask students if they know a family member or expert who may be able to contribute. You could call them, too! And don't forget about FaceTime and Google Hangouts, because video adds another layer of engagement!

- **Online curations.** Use tools like LiveBinders, eduClipper, Symbaloo, Google Docs, Diigo, or a slew of other services that allow you to save internet resources. Find resources related to the topic you're currently teaching and share them with students as additional resources they can use for their learning. Students might also know valuable resources, and it's important to let them be contributors as well as consumers. During instruction, and depending on connections, prior knowledge, and brainstorming, you may want to instantly add resources to your curated materials for the sake of keeping them dynamic and current. Note that a curation is different than a collection. Collections are everything you find. Curations are the meaningful things that, with reflection or explanation, you distill from the collection.

## WHAT YOU CAN DO TOMORROW

- **Build your Opportunibox.** You're going to need to investigate and begin playing with web tools that allow you to engage in opportunities for quick teachable moments. They include the ones mentioned above or any others that might serve similar needs. If you need a place to get started, search for "Digital Learning Strategies LiveBinders." There, you will find a variety of tools to start investigating, including tutorials on how to use them. Just a reminder that you don't have to know everything about these tools to start using them, nor do you have to be the lone expert. Your students can co-navigate this with you, and you can teach each other what you learn as you try out new tools. The teachers aren't the only ones who need an opportunity toolbox—the students need it, too!

- **In the news... (or the weather).** Who out there is teaching geologic systems or plate tectonics right now? On April 5, 2018, CNN.com shared an article entitled, "Big Crack Evidence East Africa Could Be Splitting in Two." The article shared that a huge crack in the Earth's surface suddenly appeared in Kenya, causing a highway to collapse. It was accompanied by seismic activity in an area known as East Africa's Great Rift Valley. The article was chock full of domain-specific vocab and concepts that would align nicely with what teachers might be teaching. There were additional images from CNN, links to maps that showed where in the world this was, and what will eventually happen to Africa if this eastern section breaks away from the main continent, creating a new land mass between Africa and Madagascar. It was exciting to read about and to see all the associated media. If we were still in the classroom, it would have been our lead exploration of the day! Much that comes up in news is learning-worthy. Some news stories, like this one, prompt investigations, lead to other resources, and inspire questions that might not have happened otherwise.

- **Instant field trips.** As students are learning, listen for connections, misconceptions, conversations, questions, or anything that would launch an opportunity for an exploratory pause. This is a great time to model quick research and how to come back to a task. Or to use new tech like Google Cardboard to visit places or have a virtual or augmented reality experience. Our eleven-year-old was recently learning about ancient civilizations. We contacted the teacher and asked if we could join one of their social studies classes and bring our Google Cardboard headsets. We encouraged other students to bring their headsets if they had them, and their phones, with their parents' permission. We showed them how to download Google Street View and access interesting points around the globe. In this class, we looked specifically at ancient civilization sites through Google Cardboard, which allows 360-degree views, most of which you could navigate through using direction arrows built into the app. Google also has an app called Google Expeditions, where teachers can create virtual field trips and narrate them as students move through the virtual and augmented-reality scenarios. Isn't this a great time to be a learner?

• **Generate moments of anticipation.** You can do things in the classroom like drop hints for upcoming content or activities the way HBO marketed their popular *Game of Thrones* series. Their simple marketing slogan was, "Winter is coming." They've milked this slogan for years, as it helps stir viewers into a frenzy when accompanied by a single image, such as a dragon, a boat, the king of the White Walkers, or the Hall of Many Faces. Fans were hungry for the next installment of the series and ate it up accordingly. To introduce a unit on plate tectonics, Mike used to write the word JOGA on the whiteboard a couple of weeks before the unit was to start. Students would start asking questions, and Mike would reveal very little. By the time the unit was ready to begin, the students would be absolutely ravenous to receive it. (FYI: *Joga* is a song by the Icelandic singer Bjork. Iceland sits on a divergent plate boundary, and the video for the song is a brilliant launch for learning about plate tectonics!) As another example, Liz was preparing to share a guided reading book with her class, a short novel entitled *Three Days* by Donna Jo Napoli. Liz animatedly told the class a story about a girl traveling with her father in a foreign country. The girl's dad has a heart attack and she flags down a passing car for help. Rather than

help her father, the people in the car kidnap the girl, and then they...
Well, Liz just couldn't tell the students any more, because it was too
suspenseful. Guess which students struggled with getting into the
book? That's right. None of them.

## FINAL THOUGHTS

Teachable moments ramp up the wonder and awe that should be a part of many, if not all, learning experiences. Those moments create emotional connections to the learning that virtually guarantee that students will never forget what they've learned. We need as many of these teachable moments as possible, even if we have to create them!

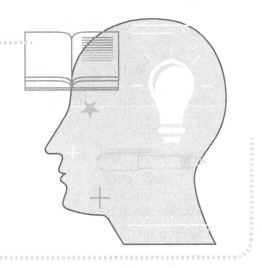

## HACK 15

# THINK LIKE A KID

## Ask yourself if you would want to be in your classroom

### THE PROBLEM: TEACHERS DON'T THINK LIKE THEIR STUDENTS

A COUPLE OF YEARS ago, we surveyed local students across Erie, Orleans, Niagara, Monroe, Genesee, and Chautauqua Counties about what they saw as working in education. We used a Google Form to capture their answers to the following questions:

1. What is working in education right now?

2. If you could make only *one* change at school right now, what would you change?

3. What else would you like to see change at school?

4. How do you like to learn?

Here is a sampling of their responses (paraphrased):

- They like hands-on opportunities.

- They like learning with peers in groups or in pairs.

- They like using technology and see it as something that is working in education.

- One student wrote that he or she wants to feel safe and be able to trust the teachers.

- One student wrote that he would like for someone to ask him about his opinion.

- "I think the technology helps a lot in schools, and having the teachers know how to work them instead of wasting the whole period fumbling around trying to understand the technology."

- They like having clubs for different subjects to extend the learning for interested students.

- "I personally like teachers that don't stop or rest until you understand and can do it over and over again correctly."

- "I would change some of the classes students have to take, like health. I took it in 7th grade, and now in 8th grade, I think if you already took the class, you shouldn't have to take it again. I know all this stuff from 7th grade, why should I have to learn it again?"

- Fewer lectures!

Note that we culled these from more than ninety responses. In general, we thought the responses had a positive tone. This was not a scientific survey, nor was the sample of respondents that broad, but we did like that students participated and were honest about what they thought. The responses were also fairly specific: They want teachers who think more like students and think about what their students would want.

The problem here lies in whether you would want to be a student in your own classroom. Are you doing things that your students care about? Are you making the best use of your resources and your space? Do you have emotional connections to every kid? If you're not doing these things, how can you expect your students to be invested in your classroom or the learning they are expected to do?

## THE HACK: THINK LIKE A KID

We're not being flippant when we ask if you would want to be a student in your classroom. We're hoping to launch a conversation that invites you to analyze your space and your instructional practices. Thinking like a kid means inviting motivation, energy, and engagement back into something that may have settled into a level of sameness or stagnation over the years. If we had a nickel for every time we heard that "these lessons or units have worked with students for years," then we'd be very wealthy. The kids of today are not like the kids of yesterday, and we have to plan for their buy-in. We have to care about their world. We have to stay loyal to the learner.

We found a few illuminating discoveries in the responses we collected; conclusions we drew as a result of what the students said, including:

- Students want us to value them for their experiences and be voices in curricular decisions.

- Students want to go beyond a comprehension level of knowledge. They want to engage with their content on a deeper level.

- Students want someone who really cares about them and their learning.

We think educators need to place more emphasis on the students' voices in all this talk of school improvement and reform. We also think we need to have the conversation based on populations of kids in our actual schools rather than trying to set national goals that only a fraction of our schools can realistically reach. We need to consider the improvement of teachers rather than putting our energies into ridiculous measures and evaluations that don't paint an accurate picture of teacher performance—or classroom effectiveness.

We need to look at our learning spaces and instructional practices through fresh eyes—the eyes of the kids—and ask ourselves questions such as:

- In what other ways could I teach what I am teaching?

- How can I invite students into the planning of both instruction and assessments?

- How deeply do I want my students to learn, and what am I willing to do to make that happen?

- Do students have real ownership of their learning in my classroom?

- Do students feel that I care for them?

- Do students freely communicate their wants and needs, and do I respectfully receive them?

- Am I here because I love teaching kids and doing whatever it takes to help them learn?

- How can I support psychological safety for my students, where they feel valued as genuine contributors?

## WHAT YOU CAN DO TOMORROW

- **What would Josephina think?** Describe a perspective analysis through the eyes of one of your current students. Is she listening to you? Are you the only one teaching? Is she listening to her peers? Does she contribute insightful information, or surface-level regurgitations? Does she seem to be interested and engaged? Does she seem excited? Does she meet tasks with groans or enthusiasm? Is she asking driving questions? Is she doing good work and good thinking? Does she feel cared for in your classroom? Are you building relationships with every student? You might not see potential problems or improvement areas unless you're looking at the situation through your students' eyes.

- **Talk to your students.** If they don't learn it your way, what other ways are there? Invite student input into the way you run your class—from classroom procedures to instructional activities to assessments.

Let them have some say and choice in what happens to them and how they learn.

- **Use affective surveys.** Use surveys that help you gauge student interests and impact. This is critical for building personal relationships with your students. Ask about personal information that will help you stay relevant to students' interests within a topic or theme. Find ways they like to learn and ways they don't like to learn. Discover what matters to them outside the classroom and leverage that for experiences inside the classroom. Affective surveys yield information for personalizing and humanizing instructional practice. We once had a sixth-grader who was behaviorally challenged, and it seemed like nothing we did had any impact on his interest, attention, engagement, or performance. When we reached the completely-fed-up point, we decided to have a one-on-one conversation with him before we pulled the parents back into the mix. It turned out he was really into boats and all things related to lakes and oceans—water sports in general; boating and waterskiing specifically. When we started related learning in the classroom to something even tangentially connected to the water, we captured his interest. It wasn't as easy as it sounds in this brief story, as we also had to deal with another dozen or so students who had the same needs for authenticity and discovering how the learning mattered to them. We stumbled at the beginning, but it didn't take long to build habits for the group of students we had that year. They allowed us to pique their varieties of interests using the little personal things we knew about them, much of which we gathered using affective surveys or having class discussions about interests.

- **Roles and identities.** In the introduction, we described potential roles for students, including explorers, performers, product managers, discoverers, champions, masters, players, evaluators, and ultimately, creators of anything imaginable. Beyond the intention for growing student identities around contemporary learning and learners, roles help students become genuine contributors and up the ante for engagement. We'll explore this notion of identity more in the upcoming Change the Channel Hack. Other roles, particularly for group work, are also important here: reader, documentarian, sketch artist, timekeeper, connection maker, link manager, video recorder, editor, devil's advocate/rule-breaker, disposition reminder, and more. Roles and identities for students in the classroom create so many opportunities for inclusion and deep learning as we remind students to think in different ways and use their voices to co-create choices for learning and deliverables.

## FINAL THOUGHTS

Teachers should know as much as possible about their students and value their opinions and contributions whenever possible. That's how you make sure you're building an environment in which *you'd* like to learn yourself—and in which students do their deepest learning.

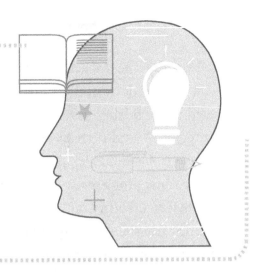

# CURRICULUM (IN)FIDELITY— LET THE CURRICULUM OUT OF THE CAN

## Be thoughtful about purchased programs

### THE PROBLEM: FIDELITY TO A VENDOR PRODUCT DISMISSES TEACHER EXPERTISE

GIVEN THE RESTRICTED time for curriculum conversations and standards analysis, many schools opt to purchase curricular materials from a variety of vendors. This, in and of itself, is not necessarily a bad practice. It becomes a problem, however, when the level of fidelity to the vendor product outweighs common sense and professional expertise.

### THE HACK: CURRICULUM (IN)FIDELITY—LET THE CURRICULUM OUT OF THE CAN

Some might argue that fidelity to a product will potentially produce research-based results. Without that level of fidelity, how do you know whether the impact is coming from the product or the teacher? We would argue, though, that if you can't tell whether the impact is coming from the teacher, there is a bigger problem. But what do you do to fix it, especially if there are administrative mandates for maintaining the fidelity in the system? How do you take advantage of a program that has precise—and perhaps constrictive—boundaries?

You have to be strategic. Talk with other teachers to find out whether they're having the same problems, and what they're doing about it. You may find opportunities, that you hadn't noticed at first, for building in scaffolds for struggling students or extensions for high flyers.

You might also want to conduct a complete analysis of the worth of each component in the program. Does the instruction meet the assessment? How is the vocabulary instruction? Are the methodologies repetitive or varied? Are the instructional strategies high-impact and increasingly cognitively sophisticated? Do you have all the resources you need?

Then take a deep look at the assessments in the vendor product. What do they measure? How do you know? *How Well* do they measure what they intend to measure? Are they recall level? Analysis level? Evaluatory? Are there opportunities to create a product of value? Are there opportunities to build new assessments, based on the vendor product, and therefore use the product in a larger way? The vendor product may guide you in creating a new assessment, but make sure you're discussing it with your colleagues first and doing it in a way that fits the students best.

> IF YOU'RE STUCK WITH A VENDOR PROGRAM THAT IS TOO RESTRICTIVE OR ISN'T MEETING THE NEEDS OF YOUR STUDENTS, GETTING CREATIVE WITH HOW YOU'RE LOOKING AT THE PROGRAM AND HOW YOU'RE USING IT CAN HELP YOU FIND WAYS TO EXPAND ON IT.

When you're done analyzing and upgrading the assessment, look to the instruction. The instruction should meet the learning needs of the students so they can perform or demonstrate what they learned on the assessment. What needs to change for students to successfully meet the new assessment? Remember to look beyond that standard, too, to account for special needs students. Does the vendor allow for teacher decisions for adapting the product? Are there scaffolds and enrichment built-in? Do those scaffolds and enrichment specifically target your students with special needs, or English Language Learners? Does the instruction meet the knowledge and thinking demands of the assessment? In short, does the instruction drive the students toward readiness for whatever the assessment might be?

You may have to go back to the standard level, too. Companies that create curriculum products often use the standards in a way that is best for their design... but not necessarily best for students. They might also align their work to a blanket standard that is hardly precise enough for a student at a particular grade level. This happens often with standards like the Common Core and its subsequent iterations. In Literacy, the standards include a set of Anchor Standards from which the grade-level standards are derived. If a vendor had trouble aligning to a standard at a particular grade level, it sometimes aligned to the Anchor instead. This either makes learning more difficult or makes learning ambiguous. Neither is a good idea. Teachers may need to go back to the standard and look at its heart: the nouns and the verbs, and how they are translated into skills and instructional actions.

If you're stuck with a vendor program that is too restrictive or isn't meeting the needs of your students, getting creative with how you're looking at the program and how you're using it can help you find ways to expand on it.

## WHAT YOU CAN DO TOMORROW

- **Look for repetitive practices in the vendor product.** Vendors often have either prescribed steps for implementing their products or a structured mechanism of delivery and assessment. This leads to repetition from one lesson or unit to another. This includes repetitive methodologies like daily exit tickets or a rote regurgitation of the day's learning. It could be the same type of assessment on the same day each week. It could be the same type of instruction on the same day each week. (Read on Monday, Organize Thoughts on Tuesday, Worksheet Wednesday, Thursday Pretest, Friday Unit Test.) It can also become like a factory model, and authoritarian. If students are going to commit to deeply learning something, their brains must form positive emotional attachments and see differences that they will remember. Analyze your products and look for repetition. If you find repetitive practices that are actively supporting student learning, keep them. If you find repetitions that aren't, or if students are struggling or losing focus and engagement because of them, take them out.

- **Don't fight the feeling.** Let your conscience be your guide when making professional decisions about vendor products. If it doesn't feel right, don't do it. If it negatively impacts your students, then stop the practice. Students' brains are quite powerful. They know whether they want to move toward the learning and engage with it. If they don't feel that pull, it could be putting students and teachers on a path of disengagement. In that case, products that were purchased to help teachers teach and students learn actually do the opposite, creating gaps in learning that are difficult to overcome as students get older.

- **Replace what needs replacing.** Be ready to think of a replacement for anything you cut out. The science behind the instructional decisions in a vendor product might not be too far off, even if the action isn't right. For instance, the purpose of exit tickets is to have a quick, informal assessment of student learning, intended to guide the teacher's actions on subsequent days of instruction. While the assessment part is absolutely necessary, the use of daily exit tickets is not. Use an oral assessment instead, a formative assessment game (perhaps student-created!), or an online assessment tool like Kahoot!, Quizlet, Google Forms, Socrative, or Poll Everywhere, or anything else that keeps the students engaged.

- **Converse, collaborate, commit.** We've said it before, and it will be a running theme throughout this text: Talk to the people you work with about curriculum and instruction. Collaborate on replacements and tweaks to the vendor product, and then commit to those decisions.

## FINAL THOUGHTS

We realize we may be poking a bear here, but we think this is a great opportunity for conversations around authentic practices. We know the reality in many schools is to adopt programs that administrators feel are right for their populations of students, and there is an expectation of buy-in and fidelity once schools implement them. What we're rallying for here is professional courtesy for teachers, and an invitation for teachers to put their professional practices before products.

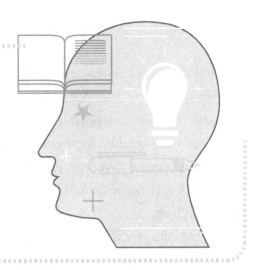

# HACK 17
# UN-COVER THE CURRICULUM
## Dig deep for maximum learning

### THE PROBLEM: TOO MANY TEACHERS JUST COVER THE CURRICULUM

MILE WIDE; INCH deep.

Teachers all over feel pressed for time and feel the need to cover the curriculum—to get the students ready for the test or to make sure they pass the test. There isn't always time to think outside the box, and many teachers ask themselves why they would bother to change when their results have always been OK.

But is OK good enough? Don't we want to improve? Don't we want to help students be the best they can be? Of course we do, but we can't do that with a "way we've always done it" mentality. As the years go by and students become savvier, coverage isn't going to cut it. And it counts for very little already.

### THE HACK: UN-COVER THE CURRICULUM

More opportunities arise for students to uncover curriculum when we give them a choice and voice in the design of their learning. Going deep with fewer ideas helps students create that mental Velcro and build a solid foundation as we discussed in previous Hacks. Depth matters more than breadth.

Going deep means making hard decisions about what to cut and what to keep in your curricular practice. This is particularly important when you consider the usage of a vendor product. Vendors will tell you that you must follow their programs with fidelity for maximum impact. (See the previous Hack!) Fidelity often translates to coverage, and students might get to a comprehension level of what we task them with learning… but that doesn't necessarily transfer to deep understanding.

To start with, we'd like to challenge you to take a critical look at your current curriculum or vendor products. Ask yourself the following questions:

- Are my students struggling with the curriculum in its current form?

- If I'm doing what is prescribed, are my students performing the way they should be?

- Am I struggling to "get through" all that is in my curriculum?

- Are there noticeable gaps between what I am teaching and any state or national assessments my students are taking? (Or in your standards in general, where some standards are overly emphasized while others are not addressed at all.)

- Do I feel like the teacher I envisioned myself being, or could anybody deliver what I'm delivering?

- Do I feel good about what I'm doing? Am I doing what is best for my students?

- Am I expected to be on the same page as my colleagues in my grade level on any given day?

The answers to these questions might give you cause to pause and reflect on yourself as a professional and the curricular resources you are using.

# WHAT YOU CAN DO TOMORROW

- **Keep it or toss it?** Many vendor products include a plethora of related materials, workbooks, or worksheets for students. Decide right now not to use them all. Be strategic and make "UN-covering" decisions based on student readiness and demonstrated performance. In *Curriculum 21* by Heidi Hayes Jacobs, she advocates for conversations around: What do we cut? What do we keep? And what do we create? Ask yourselves the same questions. If students mastered multistep equations in class and can solve them independently, they don't need four more days or six more worksheets just because the vendor says it would be a good idea. Sure, you could keep an activity or a worksheet or two for any student who feels they need extra practice before a more formal assessment, but when everyone is ready, move on. Cut the rest. Likewise, if something is super important and builds on prior knowledge, or is essential to the next concept and associated practice is necessary, keep it rather than cut it. Put your professionalism back to work and make those critical decisions. The vendor doesn't know your students.

- **Pay attention to students' questions.** They provide teachers with invaluable information that may be outside of your current curricular goals. Their questions can lead the learning down unintended but important paths toward opportunities that might not have happened otherwise—and will likely not be in the vendor program. (See the upcoming Hack on Teachable Moments!)

- **Eliminate the fluff.** We're always amazed when we see the regularity with which some vendors over-use instructional or assessment strategies. Brain-based research isn't anything new, but it still seems to be largely ignored in the educational ether. As educators, as learners, and as professional development specialists, we know that anything rote or anything that has a same-old/same-old feel to it will have virtually no impact. However, when we tell stories, invite questions, mix up the presentation, move around, and learn in a new space or in a new way, we have higher engagement—because we're keeping our audience's attention with differences. If we've got high engagement and high attention, then we're more likely to have high levels of learning and performance. As reflective practitioners, we need to look at where we're losing engagement and make the decision to let it go if it's not working.

## FINAL THOUGHTS

We strongly advocate for teachers to set their curriculum free! There are many Hacks here that extend the message of this Hack and help teachers UN-cover the curriculum by inviting student voices, exploring and discovering with students, and inspiring wonder in the classroom. We've always had a mantra of *doing what is best for kids*, even early in our careers. UN-covering the curriculum and going deep into conceptual-level learning is doing your best for your students.

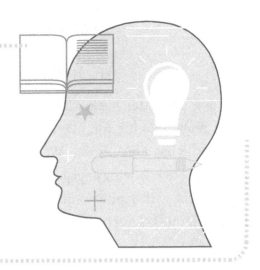

# GO DEEP WITH VIGOR

## Discover that it's not as rigorous as you think it is

### THE PROBLEM: RIGOR MIGHT NOT MEAN WHAT YOU THINK IT MEANS

RIGOR HAS BECOME one of the key educational buzzwords in the last few years. Vendors have homed in on rigor as a selling point, highlighting the term to market their wares. The bigger the company, the more intense the rigor—or at least that's what they'd have you believe. There's big money in being the most rigorous version of standards-based materials available. However, the real problem is that these products aren't necessarily as rigorous as they think they are. There's a big difference between more work and *better* work.

Take a look at what you're using or what your school is considering when it comes to vendor products. Does the product rely heavily on a strategy or type of formative assessment, such as close reading on each page of a story, or more practice with mathematical problems, or more comprehension questions than there were in previous iterations of the resource? Do its prescriptive steps negate the need for you to have a teaching degree to deliver the material? Are the materials geared toward a generalized audience of students?

That's not rigor. That's just more stuff with a side of distrust in your abilities.

## THE HACK: GO DEEP WITH VIGOR

This is a one-letter hack. Change the "r" in rigor to a "v." "Vigor" is the word you're really looking for. We know it's just semantics, but sometimes changing little things has a big impact. We're seeking opportunities for depth. We're seeking authentic growth with engagement. We don't think depth, authentic growth, or engagement will happen when we focus so intently on rigor—a word that connotes strictness, severity, and stiffness.

> SKILLS ARE IMPORTANT, BUT SO ARE
> IMAGINATION, CREATIVITY, AND INQUIRY.

Vigor, conversely, connotes robustness, health, strength, and hardiness. It makes us think of dynamic and enthusiastic learning, of interactive and innovative learning experiences, and of organic and authentic learning moments. Vigor is a word that makes us think of the joy in learning—perhaps the joy *of* learning. We've written much over the years about engagement in the learning process. You can't have real learning if you don't have real engagement. Students need an emotional anchor. They need something to connect to that they are likely to remember. Vigorous learning experiences provide those anchors for real learning.

This means that we need to consider the vigorousness of our curriculum in light of vendor products and time-honored classroom traditions. Skills are important, but so are imagination, creativity, and inquiry. We should never separate them.

## WHAT YOU CAN DO TOMORROW

- **Appraise your current week's curriculum.** Take out this week's plan and look for items that are invigorating and items that are the monotonous same-old/same-old. Replace anything boring with something more exciting. For instance, if math practice consists of a worksheet or an often-used strategy, switch it up with manipulatives. Call out a number and ask students to use the manipulatives to create visual equations as quickly as possible for fluency and processing practice. Use pennies, buttons, checkers, or anything you've got. If your students are drawing angles or shapes, what about a field trip around the school to take pictures of the angles or shapes you're studying? Come back to the classroom and organize the pictures. Use rulers and protractors to measure the images and compare what you collected. Instead of students taking traditional spelling or vocabulary tests, encourage them to use the words to tell stories orally first, then ask them to write down as much of the stories as they can remember, maybe using a digital tool like Storybird or Google Docs. Be sure to add visuals for maximum interest and engagement for the audiences that will read their stories.

- **Share your intentions.** Let your colleagues or teammates know what you're thinking and look for opportunities to share vigorous practices. Talk regularly with your grade-level or content-area team about your engagement strategies for the coming week. Share your plans and create opportunities to brainstorm about each other's work.

- **Ask the students.** In the 21st century, student voice and input is essential to buy-in and real learning. Provide your students with opportunities to make decisions about how they will learn and demonstrate their learning. Pay attention to how those choices positively affect their learning, and determine which choices help students do their best work. Students need to know that their voices are heard and valued. They need to know that their opinions matter and that they have choices in the way they learn something and how teachers will assess them.

- **Make learning fun again.** Let's get back to what really matters in learning. Vigorous learning makes acquisition and application of knowledge so memorable that teachers can virtually guarantee that students will never forget what they've learned/participated in/created. Vigorous learning spans differentiations, includes everyone's unique contributions, and gives kids the voices they need. If they are participators (such as through action, design, and conversation), then they are learners. Purposeful design and purposeful practices make the learning stick.

## FINAL THOUGHTS

Vigor, like differentiated practices, doesn't mean heaping on more work. It means finding ways to engage students in opportunities for deep, rich learning. "The way we've always done it" won't work anymore, and neither will putting a fresh coat of paint on a traditional practice. We must reimagine contemporary teaching and learning, and what it means to be instructionally vigorous.

# ENGAGEMENT
## HACKTIONS

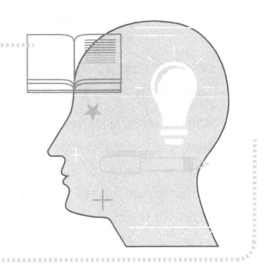

# GO ALL-IN WITH THE ABCs OF ENGAGEMENT

## Learn the necessary art of an "all-in" mindset

### THE PROBLEM: TEACHERS MISTAKE COMPLIANCE FOR ENGAGEMENT

TEACHERS OFTEN MISTAKE engagement for compliance in the classroom: students looking up, nodding heads, and "doing the work." But true engagement is more than just doing what is expected as a student. Teachers who plan activities and experiences that raise the level of concern among students hit the sweet spot. Do you have structures in place so that you might call on anyone at any time to explain, elaborate, define, or defend? Do students feel emotionally safe in their learning environment? Are students bored or frustrated with the work? Or are they fully engaged?

### THE HACK: GO ALL-IN WITH THE ABCs OF ENGAGEMENT

Engagement lives in the curiosity, passion, and concern that students have about their learning. As teachers, we need to be aware that there are three types of student engagement: **affective**, **behavioral**, and **cognitive** (the ABCs of engagement).

- **Affective** engagement deals with the emotions: Do students have connections to the school, teachers, peers, and/or topics?

- **Behavioral** engagement deals with whether students know the structures and procedures for working in the classroom. For instance, if you ask students to "Turn and Talk," do they know what the purpose of that is, and how to perform it effectively? Do they know what you expect of them? Do they know how they are progressing?

- **Cognitive** engagement means that students are working with tasks that are challenging, attainable, and yet meaningful.

When designing curriculum, teachers will want to pay close attention to all three. Outside of a specifically diagnosed special need, we can likely trace disengagement back to an issue with one of the three ABCs of student engagement. Addressing those problems can positively impact how students engage with you as a teacher, and with the learning they're doing in your classroom.

# WHAT **YOU** CAN DO TOMORROW

How do you know if your students are engaged or not? Pay attention to their behaviors. What do you see and hear? This might become some of the most valuable formative assessment data you can use.

If students say they are bored, or moan with frustration, you may need to change the cognitive load of the task, especially if changing the thinking required for a task increases their interest. If students are quiet or prefer to work alone, incorporate relationship-building activities. If students are off-task in groups or partnerships, you might want to reconsider the structures you are implementing for that experience. Beyond that:

- **Relationships matter** (affective engagement). Do you know something personal about each of your students? Do your students know each other? Do they know something personal about you? Take the time to build relationships. Personal connections, cultural responsiveness, and inclusive mindsets help students build positive environments for learning. When students feel supported, valued, and integral to the way the classroom works, they become more willing to be attentive, work harder to achieve goals, and take personal pride in their accomplishments.

- **Build respect and rapport with a "we" mindset** (behavioral engagement). Interpersonal relationships matter so much in the classroom. Model desired behaviors and interactions and let students practice what those interactions look like… and what they *don't* look like. Let the students be as accountable to each other as they are to the teacher, and develop a "we" mindset. We talk about dispositions like Habits of Mind in other parts of this book, and there are a few that specifically address the development of a "we" mindset, including thinking interdependently, being empathetic, communicating with clarity, and finding humor. The "we" mindset helps students become more prolific, more precise, and happier when they are learning.

- **STEAM, coding, and making** (cognitive engagement). There is a push in schools to get these choices integrated into the curriculum. We'd like to caution that just dropping them in for the sake of having them often leads to opportunities for enrichment, even novelty-level experiences. Those aren't bad, per se, but we're looking for the engagement that precedes deep learning, and something that helps students grasp and hang on during the learning. All these models for exploring and creativity are massively important, but like technology, we should use them with an objective in mind, rather than something to complete that has no larger purpose. The throughline with all these models is the ability to think and make decisions. You can engage these tomorrow by:

- Turning a rote process into an opportunity to create something. Think camp crafts: How can you engage students with easily available materials to create a unique product related to the learning?

- Looking at the engineering practices in the Next Generation Science Standards as they invite conversations around science, engineering, and technology. Students can model their thinking, ask and answer questions, analyze and interpret data, construct explanations and design solutions, and engage in argument from evidence.

- Reviewing the many products and processes associated with coding: thinking differently about something, building self-confidence when creating something that works, finding opportunities for new perspectives on problem-solving, learning computational thinking and logic, and thinking beyond-the-box. Check out code.org for more information and resources.

These are all zones of tinkering and trying things out to see what works and what doesn't. As such, they are valuable in the classroom when it comes to getting and keeping kids engaged. Just make sure you connect them to your overall objectives.

- **Instructional technology** (opportunities for all three types of engagement!). Using technology, such as different types of devices, websites, and apps, can engage students like nothing else does. It captivates through all types of engagement. In this day and age, students are coming to school already savvy about technology, and they are device-agnostic. They can use anything. That doesn't mean they can use it well, or that they necessarily know which technology or application is right for a particular task. Based on Michael's previous book from ASCD, *Digital Learning Strategies*, ask yourself the following questions when making decisions about using technology in the classroom:

- Is there a focus on the learning objective? Using tech for the sake of using it doesn't do much to help students have high levels of engagement or deep levels of learning. They may be engaged in the idea of trying something new, but if that something new doesn't support the deep learning around your intended objectives, then the engagement will be fleeting, and it will be difficult to regain it.

- Are there enough devices and applications to go around? Equity matters here. If you don't have enough devices, or if you depend on students to bring their own when only some have them, then equity is an issue. Make sure that if you don't have enough devices, you consider how they can work collaboratively so that each small group has a device or two. Lack of resources is a quick path to disengagement and roadblock-building.

- Did you ask students about the technology? This is a missing step in most classrooms where the teacher makes all the decisions about technologies and applications. This is also a good time to ask the students which devices they prefer, and which applications might be good for learning. Embrace their ideas, particularly ones that will deepen the learning experience and help you meet your objectives.

- **Get outside of the classroom and into authentic experiences** (opportunities for all three types of engagement!). Partner with local businesses, museums, or research firms to get your students out of the classroom and into real-life situations. Make calls to potential partners and ask to speak with their educational programming representatives. Work together to create the type of experience you would like your students to have. As a class, visit the partner you are collaborating with and direct students to take field notes. Create opportunities for them to work with representatives of the facility to add value to existing processes, artifacts, and exhibits. Take the students back to school to conduct research, take more notes, and write up what they learned. Later, ask them to combine their field experiences and what they learned and design an engaging, on-site presentation at the place they visited. Invite students' families and friends to attend. This promotes community partnerships and emotionally empowering anchors for learning with your students. Add to that the fact that these partners want visitors just as much as you want to provide meaningful, authentic tasks for your students—and it's a win-win for everyone.

## FINAL THOUGHTS

The all-in mindset around the different types of engagement needs to be considered at all times in planning and instruction. Students need constant reassurance that their ideas and work matter, that they can interact appropriately with others, and that their educational experience is pushing their thinking in multiple and various ways.

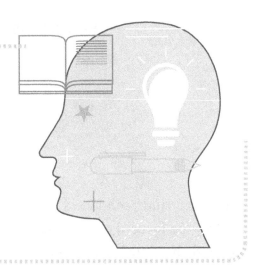

# HACK 20

# GIVE THE GIFT OF CREATIVE FREEDOM

## Create opportunities for creativity and creative problem-solving

### THE PROBLEM: AUTHORITARIAN STRUCTURES ARE STILL PERVASIVE IN EDUCATION

WHEN WE STARTED writing this Hack, Sir Ken Robinson's TED Talk on "Do Schools Kill Creativity?" had been viewed more than fifty million times. We're betting it's safe to say that many of you reading this have seen it. If you haven't, go see it now, and then come back to this Hack.

Robinson recorded this TED Talk twelve years ago. It has been discussed widely and researchers have conducted studies to quantify the decrease in creativity in recent years, including a famous study in 2011 of 300,000 people by Dr. Kyung Hee Kim, an associate professor of educational psychology at The College of William and Mary. She found that creativity has been decreasing in the United States since 1990, particularly in kindergartners through third-graders.

## SCHOOL SHOULD BE THE LAUNCHING PAD, NOT THE EXTINGUISHER.

A related study conducted in 1995 in Albany, New York, by Erik Westby and V.L. Dawson focused on the discrepancy between teachers' ideas of a creative student and the actual personality of a creative student. Their findings suggested that our understanding of creativity is one-dimensional, while creativity is multidimensional. Teachers who subscribed to the more authoritarian mindset and associated structure did little to encourage creativity the way that teachers who allowed students a greater autonomy in the classroom did.

Despite these findings, we still default to our standard models: come in, sit down, behave, do what you're told, learn what we say, take the test, graduate, and go to school or work. We're not really teaching our students if we are continuing to engage in methods popular in 1955.

School should be the launching pad, not the extinguisher. Education shouldn't kill innovation.

## THE HACK: GIVE THE GIFT OF CREATIVE FREEDOM

Encourage wild thinking and help fuel curiosity. Throw the rote away, along with the worksheets and the workbooks. Ignite a creative freedom in your classroom that's not been there before. Give students permission to think and try things out and be out-loud learners. Give them the gift of autonomy and decisional capital—where they not only get to engage in choices, but also decide what those choices will be. Redefine your classroom as a discovery zone, not a place where students come so you can gift them with knowledge. It's not a gift if they don't own it or can't receive it. And if they are going to own it, they need to discover it for themselves with support from the teacher for bridging connections, asking probing questions, and helping them understand the *Why* of what they are learning.

# WHAT YOU CAN DO TOMORROW

- **Employ a creative problem-solving method.** In the 1940s and 1950s, Alex Osborn and Sid Parnes created a procedure first known as the Osborn-Parnes Process, later renamed the CPS (Creative Problem Solving) Process. In the original version, Osborn and Parnes identified six steps to creative thinking:
  - Identify a goal or challenge or wish.
  - Gather data to help understand the challenge.
  - Ask questions about the challenge and sharpen awareness of the challenge.
  - Generate ideas that could be solutions or answers to those questions.
  - Choose the best ideas and generate potential solutions or answers.
  - Make a plan of action for meeting the challenge.

  Later, this became the four-step CPS Process:
  - Clarify
  - Ideate
  - Develop
  - Implement

  Another method is the Torrance Incubation Model (TIM), developed by educational researcher and scholar of creativity E. Paul Torrance. His three-step process is:
  - Step 1: Heighten Anticipation—Getting the students warmed up and ready to receive the new learning. (See the Hack on Teachable Moments for anticipation-level events.)

- Step 2: Deepen Expectations—Like in the Osborn-Parnes processes, this is where students define what they are doing, gather data, and generate ideas.

- Step 3: Extend the Learning/Keep It Going—This is the unique application level where students continue the learning based on what interested them in the process so far and go beyond what the teacher planned.

- **Eliminate failure.** Much learning lives in making mistakes. Don't penalize mistakes; celebrate them. They are the best ways to achieve deep learning and success, especially if students are supported with a mentality of "not yet," spurring them to maintain motivation and perseverance until they solve the problem, discover the key information, or save the world.

- **Don't be a creativity snuffer.** Fuel curiosity by inviting divergent and convergent thinking into your instruction. Divergent thinking means supporting students in generating as many ideas as possible, no matter how plausible. Convergent thinking means allowing students to bring together the best ideas to create something new or original. In the past, we've worked with students in competitive creativity opportunities like Destination Imagination and Odyssey of the Mind. The central tenets of these programs are to ask students, "How creative can you be?" and "In what ways can you be creative?" There are no right answers to these questions, but they launch a creative thinking process that asks students to be divergent first. In the execution of their tasks (with little or no parameters), what are different solutions, types of materials, and ideas for engineering a product? Then we ask them to take the best ideas and try them out, effectively creating a creativity sandbox, and merge the best ideas for the best possible outcome, and potentially a win in the competition. We need more of this type of learning in every classroom, as often as possible.

- **Launch learning with discovery-level events.** Don't give the learning away when new learning is starting. Provide students with a variety of media, including text, computers, videos, images, podcasts, and music and set a purpose for finding something. Better yet, give small groups of students something different to discover and then ask them to brainstorm connections before you start teaching anything. Be a guide on the side and support them if they come up with misconceptions, and gently ask probing/supporting/coaching questions to keep them engaged in their research.

- **Bring in the arts.** Like we mentioned in the Multimediate Hack, students need a variety of media experiences for deep learning to occur. Likewise, bringing in a variety of arts stimulates thinking and gives them enriching experiences. This includes visual arts, theater arts, musical arts, media arts—all the arts! Bringing in the arts opens doors for multidisciplinary experiences and cultural relevance that help the students' brains hold on to learning in an active and intentional way. There is a lot of critical thinking and creativity in artistic endeavors. There's also a lot of math, science, history, and literacy in artistic endeavors. Merging the learning with arts makes sense because it turns humdrum activities into performances, installations, recitals, artifacts, and new media.

## FINAL THOUGHTS

Creativity, besides serving as an essential component in the learning process, is also a key 21st-century skill. Every opportunity that educators can take to embed creativity into the learning process pays off big when it comes to retention and performance, enabling future successes and engagement as students get older. This is especially effective when an entire learning organization agrees on creativity as an essential part of its instructional ecosystem.

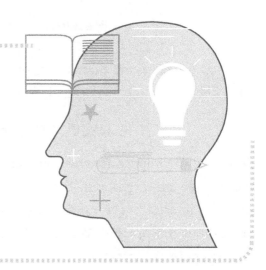

# HACK 21
# GENERATE INTEREST CURVES
## Discover and explore to re-engage curiosity and deep learning

### THE PROBLEM: TOO MANY TEACHERS STOP AT THE HOOK

**W**HEN YOU RIDE a roller coaster, your first decision is to get in line for the ride. This is an interest entry point. Then you board the ride and it begins. As you climb the first hill, your anticipation increases your interest, and your adrenaline. Going over the first hill is the thrill, but then just when the thrill starts to wane, you start going up again, then down, then around a curve, and upside down. And then, when you think the ride is over, there's one more hill, or drop, or spin, or flip. You exit the ride exhilarated and ready to ride again.

In his book about game design lenses, *The Art of Game Design*, author Jesse Schell describes this as an interest curve. There's an entry point, followed by more rising action than falling action, and everything ends with continued interest, moving the participant on to the next roller coaster ride—or the next learning event. We think this is a great way to think about learning, and guess what? It's not new.

We used to call this "the hook," assuming that once they were hooked, students would remain interested, curious, and motivated to learn. Over the years, however, teachers have diluted this process to *just* the hook, without much follow-up to keep the students engaged. And that just doesn't work.

## THE HACK: GENERATE INTEREST CURVES

We'd like to propose that we put that curiosity and engagement back into the learning equation through discovery and exploration, which are two ways to keep the interest curve up and leave students with a sense of awe and wonder throughout the process. We actively seek opportunities for creating and maintaining more rising action in our instructional endeavors. This way, we design instruction that is constantly reinviting the learner back into a zone of engagement throughout the learning process.

## WHAT YOU CAN DO TOMORROW

- **Look for the rising interest in your current curriculum documents or written lesson experiences.** Identify your hook, and then all the engagement actions in your unit or document. If there are too few engagement actions, what else can you add? Where can you build rising engagement or anticipation for the next bit of knowledge? How are students contributing their voices to instructional actions to help keep them interested and motivated? Is your lesson experience more like a thrilling roller coaster... or a flatline in need of defibrillation?

- **Identify areas of waning interest in your current documents or instructional actions.** Along with the previous bullet point, identify the spots in your plans where you know interest is waning, and replace them. When do students groan? Where do they lose interest? Is a worksheet or a checkoff list really the best way to practice a new skill or understand a new concept, or could you do something more intriguing? Are you testing on Friday because it's Friday, or because the students are ready? Are you giving more feedback than grades? How are students progressing? Are they doing the least amount to get by, or are they in it to win it?

- **Constantly look for ways to build interest or anticipation.** This is especially important during the lesson experience as, over time, it has disappeared. Most teachers are pretty good at setting the tone for learning and exciting their students, but too often it's just that one moment, and then things fall back into the "way we've always done it." Sneak mystery into your instructional plans. Drop in a Teachable Moment or two. Find ways to keep the students emotionally involved in their learning, and interested and engaged throughout the process. Doing this helps maintain motivation, endurance, and persistence across the learning experience.

## FINAL THOUGHTS

Teachers who pay attention to rising interest and maintain that level of interest across the span of a lesson experience, help students learn and perform better. This ties back in with the ABCs of Engagement and how teachers can focus on the Affective, Behavioral, and Cognitive levels of engagement in the classroom.

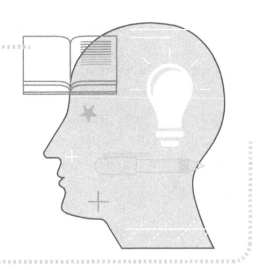

# HACK 22
# CHANGE THEIR CHANNEL
## Support student identities as learners

### THE PROBLEM: STUDENTS DON'T KNOW THEIR IDENTITIES AS LEARNERS

T HERE'S A SCENE in Pink Floyd's *The Wall* movie where students march into a machine that turns them into standardized students in desks. Each student wears the same mask and performs the same rote tasks, like walking through a maze or marching for the teacher. Sure, it's a Hollywood version of a dated English school, but how many of our students feel like one of those bricks in the wall? Like school is something they attend; where they are just numbers, in and out? Do your students see themselves as receivers of information and not actual learners?

If they do, how do we expect them to be engaged in their learning, or motivated to retain any of it? We must change the way they see themselves if we're going to lead them into deep, lasting learning.

### THE HACK: CHANGE THEIR CHANNEL

If we don't like something we're listening to on the radio or watching on TV, what do we do? We change the channel to find something more engaging and worth our time and energy. We need to help students do that. If they don't see themselves as invested in the system, we need to figure out how to *get* them invested in the system, and up the ante for engagement, learning, and performance. We do that by helping them change their channels, shifting their identities from passive receivers to specific discoverers and practitioners: such as a mathematician, scientist, writer, historian, performer, or artist.

> ## NO REAL, DEEP LEARNING WILL HAPPEN WITHOUT HIGH LEVELS OF ENGAGEMENT.

We must start thinking about instructional design that invites opportunities for students to enter these identities and maintain them throughout the learning process. If a teacher teaches a mini-lesson on multistep equations, then asks students to independently solve a problem in class in preparation to solve five more problems at home, perhaps in a workshop format, where's the interest and engagement? The moment a student loses interest and engagement, it stops the learning from getting in. We've said it before and we'll say it again: No real, deep learning will happen without high levels of engagement. This teacher, in an effort to shift the identity, could present students with a choice of problems that must be done collaboratively. These problems could be extensions of previous learning, where students individually contribute to the group's thinking and solution. The teacher asks the students what mathematicians would do if they were facing a similar problem. She reminds them to think like a mathematician; consider patterns, find connections, ask questions, and use information to piece together solutions in real-world situations. Students present their findings with fanfare, even sharing their solutions online and soliciting feedback from a global audience. Along the way, these students and their teachers are squarely focused on the process and the product, discussing multiple variations in solutions that are divergent and deeply considered.

What, then, will these students remember? The multistep equation worksheet, or the opportunity to delve into the mind of a mathematical thinker and figure out something real?

# WHAT YOU CAN DO TOMORROW

- **What would <insert content specialist here> do?** Teachers should constantly ask students what the mathematician would think. Or what the scientist would think. Or what the writer would think. Frame it as, "If you were the scientist, how might you approach this problem? What would a scientist be sure to observe? What would a scientist do with the information collected? Who would a scientist share their conclusions with?" Replace "scientist" with any other specialist. If the students are young, they may also like having the specialist title: Anna, the Mathematician. Bao, the Writer. Joaquin, the Biologist.

- **When you change the channel, consider changing the audience.** Amplify student learning by uploading student-created content to web tools that allow commenting from a variety of people around the world. You can seek feedback specifically from scientists, mathematicians, and writers by tagging them in posts to Twitter, Facebook, or Instagram, or even reaching out via email.

- **Beyond thinking like a specialist, seek reflection.** Ask your students to delve even deeper into the identities they're using for a given lesson. Ask them questions like: "How does it feel to be a scientist, an artist, a writer?" "What permissions did you give yourself to freely explore your topic?" "How did your work improve when you thought like a specialist?" "What other specialists might you need to include when you do more work around this topic?"

## FINAL THOUGHTS

Besides engaging students in the classroom, this Hack is a great way to be loyal to the learning and the students. Helping students explore and/or find their individual identities in their learning experiences creates opportunities for turning passion into action.

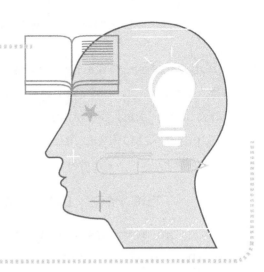

## HACK 23

# GO BEYOND ONE SIZE FITS ALL

## See why one size fits all is not reasonable

### THE PROBLEM: WE HAVE TO BE SMARTER ABOUT DATA

**E**DUCATION IS EVOLVING, and not necessarily in all the best ways. In misguided attempts to quantify every little thing and compare massive amounts of data, we're missing the primary reason we're in business to begin with: the customer. The student.

Business models aren't good for effective instructional practice. The proponents of the business model would have you believe that it is possible to quantify the learning with one high-stakes assessment that serves as an indicator of year-to-year growth, how well a teacher teaches, and whether the school as a whole is an effective system. The problem is in the variables. In science, we draw conclusions based on the testing of one variable at a time, which helps to refine the possible outcomes. In our current educational model, however, we're testing everything at once. It's bad science, and it leads to bad practices.

We're not saying that assessment is bad. Why in the world would we practice for a game we would never play or rehearse for a performance we would never give? We also don't disagree with checks and balances in the system, but the system must have integrity. That integrity lies in the priority of keeping the learner at the center. That means that we must not only find ways to assess students more rationally without causing complete psychological breakdowns on test days, but also address the other variables that the system keeps in the periphery, such as poverty, family/environmental support, and equity/fairness in instructional practices.

## THE HACK: GO BEYOND ONE SIZE FITS ALL

Think about it: In the last two decades, what has improved around curriculum and instruction? There are many exciting ways to teach and learn, and myriad ways to access all types of media. But in the last two decades, what has really changed about big/standardized assessments full of multiple-choice questions that are easy to grade but tell you virtually nothing about the learner? That's right: not a thing. Teachers are not at fault for this—but the system makes them think so by making antiquated standardized assessment methods their sole responsibility.

Raising test scores is not our objective. Teaching children is our objective.

The essence of this Hack is to simply teach extraordinarily. Teach children to go deep and justify their thinking as often as possible. Teach them to question and explore and learn what's worth learning, not just what's easy to measure. Ask students *Why* as often as possible, and then let them answer. Get back to risk-taking and making learning magic, not tragic.

Realign your thinking around how standardization impacts your instructional practice. Standardized tests are a pulse, not a diagnosis. They are meant to give a snapshot of where a student is in relation to standards, and were never meant to drive the curriculum. A one-size-fits-all test doesn't necessarily mean that we need a one-size-fits-all curriculum. That type of thinking creates a one-size-fits-*none* curriculum.

We don't want automatons in the classroom, checking off to-do lists so we can make sure we've covered as much land as possible before the assessment. Contemporary learning, in its most drilled-down state, means advocating for deeper thinking. Deeper thinking doesn't happen when we're so worried about "the test" that we feel the need to adhere, with fidelity, to what a vendor or politician tells us we should do to raise test scores.

# WHAT YOU CAN DO TOMORROW

- **Stop the test prep.** Or at least stop shutting down instruction to take a bunch of practice tests in the weeks leading up to a big assessment. Embed test-taking skills throughout the school year, and occasionally practice learning opportunities that require stamina and endurance, such as when working on research or solving involved multistep equations.

- **Build relationships.** As mentioned in a previous Hack, content matters, but caring matters a whole lot more. Do everything you can to build relationships with students, regardless of their ages, so they believe that you are on their team. Likewise, reach out to homes and families and participate in community activities. Learning is easier when students feel supported and safe. You might be the only one who treats them that way.

- **Engage in rich conversations.** Put down the worksheet and talk to students. Before students can create something new from their learning, they have to own it. That means that we have to engage in receptive teaching and learning behaviors with them. How they receive new learning is important. Having deep, Socratic-type discussions with students is a great way to engage their receptive zones so that when it's time for them to be expressive, they can do so genuinely.

- **After school/before school/during school enrichment opportunities.** For the sake of equity for all, give students the gift of differentiated experiences, even if it's just providing access to computers and books before or after the school day. Access is everything, and it is a major social justice issue. The more exposure students have to multiple perspectives, types of media, and other enriching experiences, the more likely they are to do well on assessments and move on to higher education. Let's give them that opportunity. Likewise, offering something beyond the core curriculum gives them new knowledge to work with and new connections to make, as well as allows them to explore interests that they otherwise would not have explored.

## FINAL THOUGHTS

We almost feel the need to apologize for even having to include this Hack. We know that even in our own house, our two children are as different as chalk and cheese. In schools with classrooms that have twenty, twenty-five, even thirty students, we see the potential of at least that many different experiences, not to mention the stamina and endurance that students need in order to sit for that one big test a year. It's a lot to hang on a score that might drive a bunch of decisions for which the test was not designed.

# CONTEMPORARY
## HACKTIONS

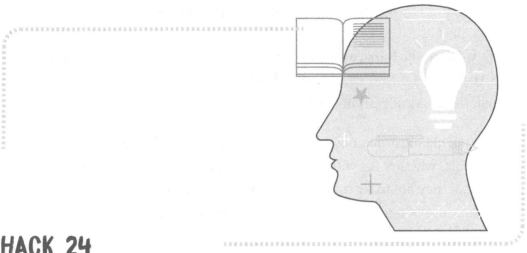

# INVITE REPLACEMENT THINKING

## Apply this notion to assessments and across other curricular elements

### THE PROBLEM: CONTEMPORARY LEARNING NEEDS CONTEMPORARY ASSESSMENTS

THESE DAYS, STUDENTS have countless opportunities to demonstrate their learning in countless ways. This doesn't mean that everything has to be digital, but it does mean that we can't continue to use the same-old/same-old paper and pencil, fill in the blank, bubble the answer, connect the dots, pop quiz Friday-styles of assessment that we have seen for decades. But so many schools and teachers still do this—and it's hampering their students' abilities to learn.

### THE HACK: INVITE REPLACEMENT THINKING

Contemporary curriculum design involves multiple facets: engaging 21st-century skills, using digital tools, collaborating with others around the globe, creating performance tasks, and more. Getting these design elements into a teacher's current curriculum demands that teachers create professional habits around replacement thinking. In short, they need to replace the dated practices with more contemporary ones.

Here we describe four considerations for replacement thinking around assessments that Michael first described in his book *Digital Learning Strategies*. In a nutshell, those considerations include:

1. Students must demonstrate what they've learned. Whatever they create, whether it's with digital tools or not, should still represent what they are to learn. The assessment shouldn't tell you more about their use of a tool than it does about their work *using* the tool.

2. Students should demonstrate content proficiency and sophistication. Their new product should reflect their content knowledge and the multiple cognitive zones they participated in during the learning process.

3. Students should frequently reflect on their choices. They should be able to articulate and defend their tool choices, content inclusion, and degrees of audience interaction, and how those choices affected the resulting product.

4. Students must give credit where credit is due. They should know about copyright, Creative Commons licensing, how to search for and use appropriate content, and how to give attribution for the media resources they use.

> ## WE CAN STANDARDIZE TESTS FROM NOW UNTIL FOREVER, BUT WE CAN'T STANDARDIZE CHILDREN.

And while assessments are the focus of this Hack, replacement thinking can apply across the curriculum in instructional strategies, classroom activities, or in formative data collection using tools such as Kahoot!, Socrative, or Google Forms. To help you start thinking about replacement thinking, we offer the following action steps to bring more contemporary ideas into your own professional practices.

# WHAT **YOU** CAN DO TOMORROW

- **Stop thinking technology first.** Instead, use the *best* tool to support learning (e.g., feedback, performance, knowledge, creativity). The task should drive the tool(s), dependent upon what the students need to do for learning. That might be to pick up a pencil, read a print text, FaceTime a student's grandma who happens to be a veterinarian in Denmark, log onto a library database, or send a tweet to find an expert on a topic they are learning about. When the tools support the learning, they are not, in and of themselves, the learning objective. Our friend and mentor Heidi Hayes Jacobs often shares a metaphor about "Crayon Labs" in schools. We don't plan to use crayons, but they are always an available option. Computer labs and digital devices are the same. They are tools in a classroom toolbox, and are always available.

- **Give students authentic choice in how they will demonstrate their learning.** Part of our charge as educators in the 21st century is to take what we know about good instruction and apply it to today's contemporary kid. We've got decades of research about how to best teach children, and much of the research intersects with instructional methods that allow for personalization of the learning process. Kids think differently and perform differently, have unique experiences, and have different ideas around what engages them. We can standardize tests from now until forever, but we can't standardize children. In fact, we should be seeking ways to develop their unique skills and perspectives for the sake of engagement, and that means offering choices in learning products, particularly if we can create those learning products with the infinite number of tools available online and on digital devices. (So long as we value the task over the tool!)

- **Help students seek feedback from other students, educators, and experts in the field.** Feedback is more powerful than grades. Let students learn to amplify. Traditional education is at a crossroads, with many things that impact the practice in a contemporary classroom. One of those things is our socially acceptable, decades-old practice around grading, much of which perpetuates desired behaviors over real learning and a punitive system of disparate generational values. Today, grades are more likely to result in roadblocks to learning than motivating students to achieve.

  So how do we grow our students without grading them? We offer them feedback about their work in the form of conversations and questions and constructive criticism. We publish unfinished drafts of their learning products online and solicit feedback from multiple audiences. We habitually amplify student work from the classroom to the world, and seek perspective analysis from other students, other educators, and experts. We teach students to consider suggestions and improve their work. Teachers could also consider using rubrics and portfolios for both assessing and collecting student work, along with all the feedback that went into the creation of a contemporary product.

  This also opens cans of worms about authenticity and work worth doing. Do we want school to be a graded checklist of the way we've always done it, or an experience that makes our students world inquisitors ready to solve unique problems?

- **Provide always-on, asynchronous access to that which is being assessed.** Everything. All the time. Access (and equity of access) is a priority cornerstone in the contemporary classroom. Access to print and digital resources is essential. Kids don't need to come to school as vessels we fill up with knowledge when they can look everything up on the internet. School needs to be the place where they evaluate knowledge, now. The *How* and the *Why* are more important than the *What*. But the *What* must always be available for every student. The task of the contemporary teacher is to help students learn to take what is now ubiquitous (knowledge), learn to filter it for relevance and quality (critical thinking), and use that to learn, grow, and demonstrate key 21st-century skills (communication, collaboration, creative problem-solving, and critical thinking—the 4Cs from p21.org). This can only happen with 24/7 access to all forms of knowledge, and that also means having real conversations about what we filter in schools.

## FINAL THOUGHTS

We need to think about our end goal. Is it to transfer knowledge, or is it to teach students to be thinkers? Is it to instill a passion for attaining goals? Do we want our students to be good at Trivia Crack and *Jeopardy!*, or do we want to give them a toolbox of opportunities that allows them to solve unique problems? Contemporary instructional practice is about letting go of past practices. Contemporary curriculum design is about inviting students to the design table and allowing them to co-create the learning experience. We should be seeking the sweet spot of learning, where the 21st-century tools and practices enhance the lesson, but are not the lesson itself.

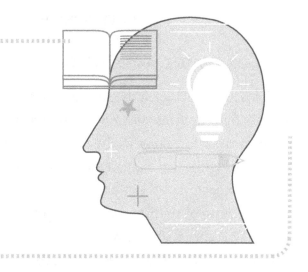

## HACK 25

# BE THE FUEL, NOT THE FLAME
## Discover why Personalized Learning isn't what you think it is

### THE PROBLEM: PERSONALIZED LEARNING IS NOT A REDUCTIVE PRACTICE

PERSONALIZED LEARNING IS quite popular in education at the moment. Teachers and administrators tout their revitalized lesson plans and online learning opportunities, but fail to see that adults are still making all the decisions. Personalized Learning is not a program, it's not a new synonym for differentiated practices, and it's not just letting students navigate an online resource without any adult guidance.

To be honest, and we're paraphrasing Ray Bradbury here, but if your students can be taught by a computer, then perhaps they should be. Personalized Learning is not meant to be reductive, and it's not a distillation of learning and technology's greatest hits. It does pair nicely with some of our other Hacks and seeks a learning experience that is co-designed with students (both student-to-student and teacher-to-students), and allows for choices in exploration, discovery, interests, and passions. It also includes voices. If you don't have student voices with your choices, then you don't have real Personalized Learning.

## THE HACK: BE THE FUEL, NOT THE FLAME

William Butler Yeats is beckoning us again. We're not filling pails, and we're not just lighting fires. What we're doing is creating the conditions in which fire can occur. Real Personalized Learning is a new ecosystem for teaching students. It involves authentic challenges, student voice, co-created learning experiences, feedback, coaching, reflection, and so much more. It does take practice, time, and a reimagining of tradition to do it right, but it makes such a difference for deep learning because it allows you to invest in student interest and motivation.

To begin, think of your Personalized Learning journey in terms of three distinct steps:

- Identify a learning goal.

- Decide with students how you might meet the goal, and what the demonstration of learning could look like.

- Decide with students what checkpoints might look like throughout the learning experience.

Now, let's flesh this out a bit:

- Identify a learning goal.

  - Here, students are contributing to what it is they want to learn and why they want to learn it. Initially, the teacher may shape it, based on standards-informed responsibilities, but students will have a hand in co-creating some of the components of the experience.

  - After the teacher establishes what the challenge is, students and teachers can unpack related standards and start working on learning targets together.

  - Teachers can help students understand what the big content pieces and skills are as students navigate how they will engage those skills across a variety of interest-based actions.

- Decide with students how you might meet the goal, and what the demonstration of learning could look like.

  - Together, teachers and students draft a proposal for what the assessment or demonstration of learning might look like, and the form it will take based on the bullet points under "Identify a learning goal."

  - From this proposal, students co-create a commitment statement for the assessment that they choose.

  - Teachers and students co-create criteria around what mastery would look like. This can take the form of a rubric or another type of narrative feedback option.

  - Teachers and students also need to make decisions about audience, and who will receive the deliverable. This is a good time for teachers to get into the habit of creating assessment opportunities that are well beyond the traditional. If the teacher is the only audience for students' work, those students might not be pressed to do their best.

- Decide with students what checkpoints might look like throughout the learning experience.

  - Teachers and students can decide on milestones and check-in points during the learning experience.

  - They should put these milestones and check-ins on a calendar, for both accountability and time management.

  - Teachers should help students seek feedback from a variety of places, such as their peers, other teachers or professionals, or vetted online contacts or mentors that have knowledge students might need.

  - Have discussions about dispositions around self-regulating, communicating and collaborating, continuous questioning and learning, metacognition, endurance, and persistence—Habits of Mind that students must demonstrate while in the Personalized Learning mindset.

## WHAT YOU CAN DO TOMORROW

- **Understand what Personalized Learning is not.** Personalized Learning is inherently a customizable learning plan that is co-created by the student and the teacher, where students, as Allison Zmuda and Bena Kallick write in *Students at the Center*, "actively pursue authentic, complex problems that inspire co-creation in the inquiry, analysis, and final product and incorporate opportunities for voice, social construction, and self-discovery." It is not individualization, where students are simply determining their own pace through the teacher-created tasks. It is also not differentiation, where students choose from a teacher-designed menu of options for learning. Note that we are not suggesting that individualization or differentiation are bad practices. Quite the contrary; there is value in having varied methodologies in a classroom, and the choices among those methodologies should be driven by tasks, time for tasks, what the assessment will (or could) be, and student contributions.

- **Invite students to contribute their ideas.** Speaking of student contributions, you can create Personalized Learning on a big or small scale depending on several factors. On the small scale, teachers can invite students to ask questions that they are interested in answering (see the Hack on Inquiring Minds) and then use those questions as a launching pad for co-creating lesson experiences and the assessment or demonstration of learning. But we don't have to stop there. In North Carolina, Charlotte Mecklenburg Schools has an entire system of Personalized Learning across many of the schools in their district, and it has demonstrated positive results. They empower students with multiple pathways for learning that are co-generated with teachers, so that students have a brand-new level of ownership over their learning.

- **Document individual student contributions.** Students in Charlotte Mecklenburg Schools also document their own Personalized Learning plans, where they provide explanations about how they will reach their goals, what processes and activities they will participate in toward their goals, and how they will demonstrate mastery. Once teachers lay a foundation for content and standards, students can start contributing goals, learning targets, and ideas for assessment. (See the Hacks on Goal-Setting and Learning Targets.) Students self-document the decisions they make and can use the templates from the Goal Setting Hack or create something new.

- **Don't just stick the student on a computer.** This is our greatest lament around Personalized Learning and what it definitely is not. There are so many programs out now that promote Personalized Learning where students sit at computers and navigate choices the way they would with a Choose Your Own Adventure book. Alfie Kohn has written about many of the online programs associated with Personalized Learning that amount to nothing more than selling technology products. Now, we're not opposed to the Choose Your Own Adventure mentality, but the students must be involved in the creation of the choices and the demonstration of learning for it to count as personalized. If they are making choices within something that's already designed, then that is more about individualization than personalization. Some of the programs do report improved achievement, and we're not knocking all of them as viable alternatives for learning everywhere (such as for home-based learning), but just sticking a kid on a computer and expecting self-directed learning and mastery is, to coin a phrase, educational laziness.

## FINAL THOUGHTS

Another takeaway from this Hack is that Personalized Learning work is incremental. Try some ideas out and see how they work. If it works, keep doing it and then add something else. We realize that there are a number of factors, including time and/or number of students, that might be potential roadblocks, but for the sake of giving students awesome school experiences, teachers should definitely consider Personalized Learning.

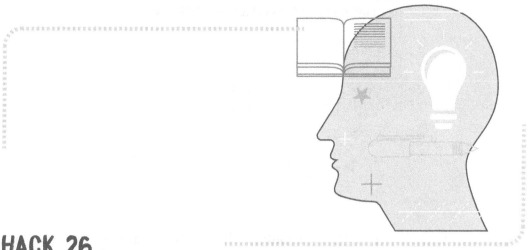

# GO BEYOND YOUR BORDERS

Take a journey to Ultima Thule

## THE PROBLEM: THE TEACHER IS STILL THE PRIMARY AUDIENCE FOR STUDENTS

T HAS LONG been standard practice that students do the work of school in the classroom. This was true when school was just one room, and it is still pervasive today. While there may be the occasional field trip, it is rare to find a classroom that is consistently amplified and globally interactive in its normal operating procedures. Outside-of-the-classroom connections are still carefully planned events rather than authentic opportunities for making the whole world the classroom. In the previous Hack, we mentioned that audiences beyond the teacher are an important part of contemporary teaching. Here, we show you how to do that.

## THE HACK: GO BEYOND YOUR BORDERS

Engage students with a journey to Ultima Thule. Ultima Thule means a far-off land, or what is beyond the known. It was a term used by ancient cartographers to indicate places that were far away, unknown, or unexplored. They noted these places on maps as "thule," meaning a faraway place, or "ultima thule," the farthest of faraway places.

> MAKE VIDEOS AND POST ONLINE, INVESTIGATE SKYPE IN SCHOOLS, EMAIL TEACHERS IN OTHER COUNTRIES, AND SHARE STUDENT WORK IN ONLINE SOCIAL/EDUCATIONAL SPACES.

In this metaphorical context, we should see Ultima Thule as a way to go beyond the known and reach a new audience target in contemporary classrooms. It begs several contemporary questions:

- How far can we reach?

- What is the impact of inviting "beyond the classroom" audiences?

- How do I create connections?

- How do I amplify student work and seek feedback from a global audience?

- How do I create "always available" opportunities for inviting the world into the classroom?

## WHAT YOU CAN DO TOMORROW

To move beyond your classroom borders, you must consider how you might relinquish some control for where knowledge lives, who owns the knowledge, and how the knowledge will be shared.

- **Begin investigating social technologies that will put you and your classroom into the world, and invite the world into your classroom.** Work within whatever safety parameters you need to, but amplify your learning! Make videos and post online, investigate Skype in Schools, email teachers in other countries, and share student work in online social/educational spaces like Edmodo, Schoology, Canvas, or blogs.

- **Start building your own network on Twitter, Instagram, or Facebook.** The larger your network, the greater your opportunity for a viable research alternative. When the research process begins for you or your students, query your network for research results that will be beyond what Google, Bing, databases, or encyclopedias might yield. Networks can bring surprises in differing views on knowledge and processes, new information that has recently become available, or compelling and essential questions to reshape or refine the research. As students get older, encourage them to build their networks too, and specifically discuss who to follow/friend in these services. Always remember to model appropriate online behavior.

- **Tear down the walls and build a new habit.** Make the historical meaning of Ultima Thule a thing of the past. For every (or at least many) new instructional action in your classroom, get into the habit of asking how interacting with the world might impact the learning. Use guiding questions like: What would a global audience think about our product? What are the consequences of inviting audience feedback from other places? How can students give actionable and meaningful feedback to others? Who else in the school might I need to get this working? Who else in the world can I invite to give students feedback?

## FINAL THOUGHTS

When audiences change, learning and performance change as well. Based on our experiences, when we hold students accountable to others beyond the classroom, they tend to do better work that demonstrates a deeper level of learning. And a bonus is that they get to interact with others and receive feedback that might help them grow beyond their own cultural and learning boundaries.

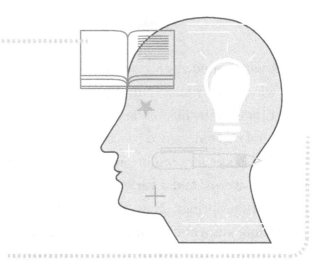

## HACK 27

# LET THE FUNCTION DEFINE THE FORM

## Explore contemporary spaces

### THE PROBLEM: CLASSROOMS STILL LOOK LIKE THEY DID FIFTY YEARS AGO

ROWS OF DESKS and chairs. The board (and teacher!) at the front of the room. Stacks of old textbooks and a teacher's desk, perhaps a podium, from which to pontificate. It is a room set up for an *obey* state—a place for people to follow directions, do what they're told, and think what they're told to think. It might sound like we're painting a mental picture of the classrooms of the 1880s or the 1930s, but unfortunately, in many places, this also describes 2018. Classrooms have not evolved in the 21st century.

### THE HACK: LET THE FUNCTION DEFINE THE FORM

There is a school in Rudrapur, Bangladesh, that is made entirely of natural materials, including bricks created locally from the surrounding alluvial sediment, straw, and bamboo. The lower level of the structure is a network of cave-like rooms with rounded entryways, and the upper floor is a wide-open space with large windows for maximum light entry.

At Erika-Mann Elementary School in Berlin, Germany, the entire interior of the school was redesigned based on student input and creativity to generate transformable spaces for comfort and maximum learning. There are couches, fold-out benches, caverns, and a variety of tactile areas.

In Clifton Springs, New York, a college prep program was designed around innovation, authentic learning, STEM, and collaborative investigations. Students are invited to learn in spaces that can be adapted in the moment for the task or conversation.

What do these spaces, and other contemporary spaces like them around the world, have in common? For one, they have the student at the center. For another, they are allowing form to follow function in a multivariate way, where spaces can be reimagined depending on the learning that will take place.

These spaces are not about indoctrination and the authoritarian design elements that have been pervasive for decades. Instead, they're about interactive zones of instruction designed to meet the contemporary needs of student explorers and their tasks.

Students need a variety of spaces in which to learn, collaborate, and think. Those spaces need to be multifunctional and provide opportunities that invite and promote deep thinking. This is not the four walls and rows of desks in classrooms of the past. In fact, let's not even call it a classroom at all. It is a learning space, and it varies with tasks and learning opportunities. Its many functions include collaboration zones, comfort zones, experimental areas, research areas, virtual training, video and presentation production facilities, and reflection spaces.

In her book *Curriculum 21*, author and educator Heidi Hayes Jacobs writes, "Most schools are not really built for children, let alone for learning. They tend to be buildings of uniform size classrooms, but all of the students vary in size at different ages. Chances are that the majority of readers of this book work in a place that has restrictions on the use of space. You have inherited a space dictated by a mindset about school design that is highly limited."

# WHAT YOU CAN DO TOMORROW

Teachers and schools can certainly purchase flexible furniture and redesign their learning spaces, but the reality is that schools have little money. We need to figure out how to do as much as we can with what we have. Here are a handful of ideas:

- **Set your desks free!** Allow students to move their desks into multiple types of groupings: small groups, circles, and pairs. If you must continue to utilize rows of desks, make sure that it is for a specific purpose and not just convenience. You may need to teach students protocols and procedures for interacting in different ways, but allowing them to create their own spaces and have their own design choices for groupings encourages motivation and buy-in. You may also need to give students a bit of time to get used to new groupings. Since they are intentionally inviting conversation and communication and collaboration, students may need time to socially navigate this new situation. As mentioned in previous Hacks, you might want to use Project Zero's Visible Thinking routines for stimulating group conversations. Creating student-generated, teacher-managed class protocols will help students understand their roles. You could also look to Art Costa and Bena Kallick's Habits of Mind for teaching students a variety of dispositions for working together.

- **Apply for a grant.** Visit DonorsChoose.org or DigitalWish.org, or search LiveBinders.com for grants that will go toward purchasing flexible furniture. Have your students write the grants! Note that in the past couple of years, some entity or foundation has sporadically sponsored every project on DonorsChoose.org. This should be an essential tool in a teacher's toolbox for getting what you need in the classroom!

- **Take an architectural walk around your campus with students.** Also in *Curriculum 21*, Jacobs advocates for architectural tours of school buildings or campuses with an eye on where learning can happen. Students will often have bold, creative ideas for ways to use spaces for different types of learning. Invite their ideas and then take action on all that you can.

- **Digital spaces matter, too.** In his book with Marie Alcock and Allison Zmuda, *The Quest for Learning*, Michael describes five different spaces that students can fluidly move in and out of: physical, plus, public, member, and mentor spaces. The physical space is the classroom and the plus space is the classroom with additional technology that launches it beyond the four walls. Most of the decisions in the physical and plus spaces are determined by the teacher. In public spaces, however, students start taking ownership. They make decisions about the online resources they will use and the way the physical space may be modified to meet their learning needs. In the member spaces, students seek out online experts or curated resources on YouTube, Pinterest, eduClipper, or LiveBinders, where they can either interact with someone who has the knowledge they need or with the resources that someone else has put together that are related to their learning needs. In the mentor space, students become the teacher and the learner. They might be the ones curating resources or be an online voice for others learning about a shared topic. In the mentor space, they learn from each other and share their learning with apprentice students who seek mastery.

## FINAL THOUGHTS

Architects and building administrators who are thinking about these sorts of spaces should ultimately think about flexibility and fluidity. We want learning spaces that invite collaboration, communication, and creative problem-solving rather than rote dispensing of knowledge in an authoritarian model that promotes "the way we've always done it" thinking.

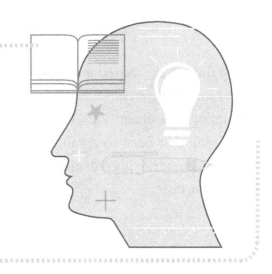

# INVITE GAME DESIGN LENSES INTO YOUR PRACTICE

## Forget what you know and reacquaint yourself with gaming

### THE PROBLEM: TOO MANY TEACHERS IGNORE GAMES AND GAME DESIGN

**W**HEN WE BROACH the topic of games in the classroom, we often see eyes rolling or yawns or flat-out fear on the faces of the educators we work with. They know that students are playing games outside of the classroom, but don't know how to make those games educationally relevant. In contemporary classrooms, teachers who care about what their students care about outside the classroom are going to be the most effective inside the classroom. That means teachers need to care about and get familiar with games and game design literacy.

### THE HACK: INVITE GAME DESIGN LENSES INTO YOUR PRACTICE

Game designers consider so many aspects of a game as they figure out how to get people to play, and continue to play, their games. They have to consider the totality of the experience and think of the player's interactions with other players and the environment. That's a lot to think about, right? But you are an instructional designer. Shouldn't you be doing the same thing? Of course you should, but you need to do so in an authentic and intentional way rather than just throwing more ingredients into your classroom bowl, stirring it, and hoping for a better taste.

GAMIFICATION INVITES TEACHERS TO THINK ABOUT FACETS OF THEIR CURRICULUM THROUGH GAME DESIGN LENSES SUCH AS JOY, FUN, CURIOSITY, MOTIVATION, JUDGMENT, ECONOMY, BALANCE, AND STORY.

Note that there is a difference between gamifying the curriculum and game-based learning. Certainly, a teacher might invite games into the classroom the way that you are thinking about them now. Students can play games to learn a skill or practice something they are in the process of learning. These may be physical or virtual games, and may include options for trying things out without penalty (sandboxes), giving them opportunities to simulate a unique situation and response, or allowing them to think critically about more generalized decisions within the game.

Gamification, though, is all about using what the game designers are using to create an experience, and we're going to apply that to instructional design in a similar way. Gamification invites teachers to think about facets of their curriculum through game design lenses such as joy, fun, curiosity, motivation, judgment, economy, balance, and story, just to name a few. Gamification might incorporate levels, badges, or achievements, and give students more choice about directions and potential choices in assessment. Gamification also invites critical thinking and creative problem-solving the way it does in game-based learning—but rather than generalized thinking, gamifying helps students drill down to whatever the intended learning goals are.

# WHAT YOU CAN DO TOMORROW

- Download **Game Design: A Deck of Lenses** app by Jesse **Schell.** These lenses are also available in book form and in a deck of cards. The app is free (and available from both Apple and Android stores) and all the lenses are available for free through the app. After you download the app, you may decide that you want the book or the deck of cards. Read through the lenses and become familiar with them. These lenses are going to help inform instructional decisions you will make based on the next few bullet points.

- **Figure out what resonates with you or your students' interests.** Become familiar with a handful of the lenses that resonate with you. Choose a variety that interest you, or share them with students and let them choose some. When you are reading the lenses, you'll notice explanations for what the lenses entail and questions that the lenses invite about enhancing your game or curriculum. Exchange the words "gamers" for students and "games" for curriculum or instructional practices in the explanations or questions in each lens you choose to engage.

- **Apply the game design lenses to your curriculum.** In what ways could you apply the lens questions to a facet of your curriculum design, either in instructional actions or in assessments? What improvements might you expect to see if you applied game design lenses to your practice? What might happen when you invite students into this conversation and let them choose lenses to apply to their learning and their products? Applying the game design lenses allows for critical thinking around singular lenses for curricular improvement. These are actual lenses that game designers use to enhance their games and improve the experiences for the players. We're challenging you to apply these lenses to instructional design to enhance your practices and improve the experiences for your students.

## FINAL THOUGHTS

Game design lenses can enhance your instructional practices the way that seasoning enhances food. These lenses provide a slew of topics to discuss and opportunities to upgrade what you already do. In fact, we think it would be a great idea for schools to look at one lens a week, or devote a month to game design lenses, where all of the professional, reflective conversations around curriculum work focus on game design lenses for upgrade inspiration!

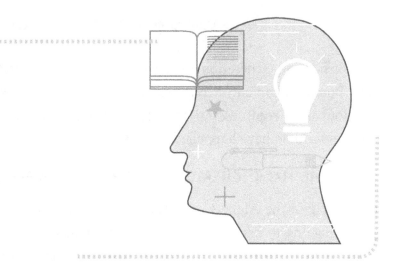

# CREATE AN ALPHA-BALANCED CURRICULUM

## Plan for what's coming next

### THE PROBLEM: CONTEMPORARY STUDENTS AREN'T INTERESTED IN TRADITIONAL CONSTRUCTS

DEPENDING ON WHEN you open this book for the first time, at least eighteen years have gone by since the beginning of the 21st century. Eight years ago, we saw the ending of Generation Z, those children who were born between 1995 and 2010. They are now in our classrooms and have been for some time. Since 2010, more than thirty million more children have been born, and they represent a brand-new generation: Generation Alpha. This generation is also known as the Global Generation or Generation Glass. They will be the most technologically literate generation in all human history. These are the children of Gen Xers and Millennials and they will live into the 22nd century.

The problem is that we haven't let go of the past. These Alphas are already in our classrooms, albeit at younger grade levels, and we're still working to get where we should have been a decade ago. We are preparing for Generation Alpha while still considering Generation Z's needs, while using Generation X's resources, and Baby Boomer's content. It boggles our minds when we walk into schools where they tout their readiness for the 21st century. We're almost 20 years in… and readiness should have happened already!

## THE HACK: CREATE AN ALPHA-BALANCED CURRICULUM

The people in the Alpha Generation, as a function of the world they were born into, are going to have very specific needs. Teachers will need to examine their curricula for opportunities to engage this generation of learners, and this includes all access to everything all the time. No more computer lab Thursdays. No more coming to school just to receive knowledge and information. No more limitations on what if or what's next.

Gen Alpha will also insist on being entrepreneurial. Think back to the Hack on Context. This is where the rubber meets the road for Gen Alphas. They will want to learn, apply, and create in many learning situations where the creation or the deliverable is relevant to other audiences—and specifically paying audiences. They will want to create content of substance and worth that they can share with the world, not just turn in to the teacher.

This generation is perfectly at home online. In fact, even the youngest members are already fluent in a multitude of devices and can search by voice for just about anything they want, from making slime to finding out how to play a new game or discovering the quickest way to clean something up that they don't want Mom or Dad to find first. Let me reiterate here: These Gen Alphas don't need to know how to read to begin searching digital devices. Traditional print literacy is no longer the main literacy entry point. (It's still super important, though!)

Gen Alphas, while a well-connected generation, will not necessarily have the same social skills as previous generations. They are comfortable and will seek out online interactors—at the expense of physical/live human interactions. Because of this, teachers will need to be cognizant of soft skills like the Habits of Mind, as well as what Michael Fullan and Andy Hargreaves describe as social and human capital.

The planned curriculum for these students should be in balance with these needs. Teachers need to care about the world their students are currently living in and the world they will graduate into. Knowing the above, in partnership with existing instructional practices, creates a contemporary curriculum that is inclusive of Generation Alpha's needs and the responsibilities of the teacher. What we've done up until now in education has worked for the majority of students. However, those methods and practices will wane in effectiveness as time moves forward.

## WHAT YOU CAN DO TOMORROW

- **Plan for 24/7 access across multiple devices.** Teachers will need to be more considerate of skills rather than content. The *What* is out there already. The *How* and the *Why* are still critically important. Devices are a requirement in the classroom, just as paper or pencils or chairs are choice items. Contemporary learners need experiences with all these materials, including different types of devices that allow for different functions: tablets for portability, and laptops and desktops for more powerful research, writing, and product-making. Note that we are not suggesting they should be *on* the device 24/7, just that those devices must be available when needed. Start planning for a way to make this happen.

- **Plan to create products of value.** Teachers will need to consider learning outcomes where students can demonstrate learning in innovative and creative ways. Students will want to create these demonstrations of learning for a much wider audience (see the Hack on Ultima Thule) and perhaps for a chance to make money or a difference.

- **Start collaborating when thinking critically and creatively.** Teachers will need to provide opportunities for digital interactions, virtual connections, making, prototyping, gaming, video production, virtual destinations, coding, and more! All of these "hot" activities in education boil down to decisions that children make and the outcomes or consequences of those decisions. These different opportunities invite students to be metacognitive, high-level thinkers who reflect on their decisions and choose more wisely.

- **Plan to teach more soft skills.** What this generation can do with technology will be mind-blowing, but many will lack skills like persistence and the ability to manage impulsivities—dispositions that are focal points in the previously mentioned Habits of Mind. With everything available all the time, students develop habits that keep them from exploring and discovering. Alexa and Siri are only going to help students to a point, and then students need to navigate learning, communication, and collaboration in ways that technology is currently eroding in human interactions. Be prepared to help them with these skills so they can move forward into the world purposefully and successfully.

## FINAL THOUGHTS

Generation Alpha, and by extension, Millennials and Generation Z, will increasingly need to see a high degree of equilibrium between their worlds outside of school and how they interact and learn inside of school.

# BLUEPRINT
## HACKTIONS

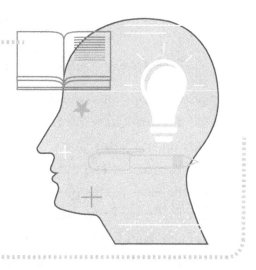

# HACK 30

# DESIGN A BLUEPRINT FOR INSTRUCTION

## Create an action plan for learning

### THE PROBLEM: TEACHERS DON'T HAVE ENOUGH EXPERIENCE WITH INSTRUCTIONAL DESIGN

MOST EDUCATIONAL PREP programs require their students/future teachers to submit lesson plans or create units as activities in their classes. Often, they follow a set pattern or Madeline Hunter format, or six-point lesson plan style. This is often done for the sake of one class in the program, and future teachers don't participate in the process again until it's time for them to student teach, or when they are actually in the classroom teaching. Unless their cooperating teacher or the school they eventually work in has an instructional design process in place, many teachers are left to their own devices for crafting maps, units, and/or lessons. That is, unless they are using a vendor product or a form of already written curriculum.

## THE HACK: DESIGN A BLUEPRINT FOR INSTRUCTION

Many of the professional development sessions and books we've experienced and read over the years have overlapping elements. A lot of that overlap lives in this book, but up until this point, we haven't explained how these elements might come together to create a curricular unit of study. While we would be thrilled if you took the ideas in this book and made dozens of blueprints for learning, there are basics that must be in every curricular plan. We're going to walk you through that base here, and then you can build just about anything on top of it!

Decide where you are going to start, whether you are writing a standards- or topic-based unit, or starting with an assessment and figuring out how to prepare students toward that assessment. You can do this with any number of already established frameworks including Universal Design for Learning (UDL), Understanding by Design (UbD), learning goals maps, or even the Madeline Hunter format. You'll need to define the content knowledge, skills, and dispositions that go along with your unit of study, and then consider how you will assess it. While we are laying out parts of the master plan here, project designers and architects know what matters most and when and how they will deviate from the basics to build a better and/or more interesting structure. To begin, these are your initial blueprint decisions:

1. Decide on the topic or at least the title of the unit or learning experience. This could also be based on an interest area from students. Imagine if students started the process by sharing what interested them!

2. Prioritize the standards that will go along with the unit or learning experience.

3. Break the standards you chose down into content and skills for what the students will have to know and be able to do.

4. Write a couple of essential questions that represent the broader goals of the content and skills in the unit.

5. Decide how you will assess the students.

These actions are the non-negotiables for every unit or learning experience you create. If you don't necessarily go in this order, it's fine. If you begin with assessments or a topic, you still need to go through the other actions to create your basic plan. If students are going to be contributors, then the teacher still needs to be the one looking for standards that fit together to form a unit of study. We're not talking about a forced fit or a loose application of standards, either. It should be something that meets both students' needs and teachers' expectations.

> PUTTING TOGETHER A UNIT OF STUDY IS NOT MEANT TO BE A *TIME*-INTENSIVE EFFORT. IT IS MEANT TO BE AN *INTENTION*-INTENSIVE EFFORT.

You can add additional blueprint decisions to this, but not necessarily *in place of* any of the initial decisions. Once you finish these actions, you can then layer in any (or all!) of the other Hacks in this book, including:

1. Create engaging learning experiences within bigger units of study.

2. Anticipate potential scaffolds, enrichments, and sophistications for students that need them.

3. Invite student voices into the mix for questions they have, words that matter to them, ideas for instructional strategies and motivation, and how they'll be assessed.

4. And speaking of words, you'll need to plan strategically for what words will require explicit instruction. (See the Hack on Morecabulary.)

5. Plan checkpoints and formative assessment opportunities.

6. Decide what resources you'll need.

Putting together a unit of study is not meant to be a *time*-intensive effort. It is meant to be an *intention*-intensive effort. With intentionality, teachers can plan unique learning scenarios that challenge students to approach unique problems, projects, and performances with wild wonder and deep attention.

# WHAT YOU CAN DO TOMORROW

- **Skip the granular lesson level.** Like we said in the Lesson Experiences Hack, granular daily lesson plans are an unnecessary practice. When you begin documenting your curriculum and putting all these pieces together, it's a better idea to spend your time on well-fleshed-out unit plans that contain all of your instructional actions, scaffolds, potential differentiation moments, and enrichment. You could document this in a single, well-planned unit, or derive it from a unit as a week-long plan. This wouldn't be much of a Hack if you spent every waking minute planning at the granular lesson level. You need that time to grade papers, right? (Kidding…) Lesson plans are too time-intensive to consider them as a contemporary professional practice. Let them go. Be more mindful about unit plans instead, where contingencies, teachable moments, reteaching, and deep learning can live in harmony with the time you have to teach. Note that in the narrative previous to this section, we wrote that you might plan for units or learning experiences. When we refer to learning experiences this way, we're referring to what we consider "lessons" plans, meaning a series of interconnected lessons that we group together as the learning experience.

- **Appraise what you have already.** Look for these elements in your currently documented curriculum. Anything missing? Do you understand all the interrelated parts? In short, do you know the *Why* behind all your curricular decisions, even if they include vendor products, textbooks, or other resources? In your appraisal, look for similarity in language across the standards, the skills, and the assessments. Is there at least a visual congruence? Look to the Hack on C.L.E.A.R. for more information about appraising what you currently have documented.

- **Draft. Then draft again. And again.** Every year is a new opportunity for revisiting and redrafting your curriculum. This is how you keep it alive.

We advocate for your curriculum to flourish—not just to live, but to be full of life—to thrive! Your unit plans and curriculum maps (covered in the upcoming Hack) are always in draft state. You will always need to reflect upon and update them. Reflect on what happened in your currently documented unit. How did the students respond? What was the level of understanding? Could you have tweaked the activity? Do you need to change your approach? Did the students learn what you intended for them to learn? Did your students and you meet the objectives? These questions, and many more like them, help to shape the next draft, the next iteration, of your unit. Doing this yearly keeps your curriculum in a constantly evolving contemporary state.

- **Be creative!** Our colleague and mentor Heidi Hayes Jacobs likens curriculum work to an act of creative writing. To meet the needs of our right-now students, we need a right-now curriculum that represents both the content and context of what we teach, and also represents the time in which we live and the world the students will eventually graduate into. Give yourself permission to go so far beyond the box of tradition that you orbit it, seeking new solar systems to join with exciting curriculum actions and enthusiastic practices. If you can invite students into that creativity, all the better!

## FINAL THOUGHTS

While we are laying out a basic blueprint as a reference, note that we stated earlier that what we offer in this book is programmatically agnostic. You should be able to apply some or most of what we've shared here within any given framework. Those frameworks will deviate from our basic blueprint, but they should be close enough for what we're sharing here to make sense. The bigger point is to use your professional expertise and knowledge, along with collegial conversations, to make the best decisions for you and your students!

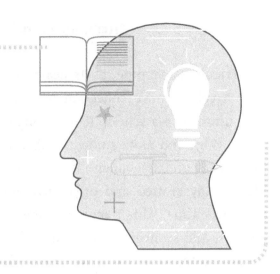

# COMMIT TO YOUR COLLEAGUES
## Map curriculum together

### THE PROBLEM: TOO MANY TEACHERS TREAT MAPPING AS JUST FILLING IN BOXES

**M**ANY DISTRICTS THAT undertake a curriculum mapping initiative end up creating a map that is an outline for compliance. It quantifies what teacher intentions are and, when completed, becomes a rarely touched shelf-filler. The map is meant to show dynamic, documented evidence of professional collaboration, as well as what the actual curriculum is. Sadly, many teachers who participate in mapping become overwhelmed with the prospect of creating it and loathe the thought of having to pore over it for analyses as a result of administrative directives. The purpose for mapping was lost in the directive to do so, and the results are often the minimum amount of documentation to complete a task.

That's not mapping; that's busywork, and as such, it is a waste of time.

### THE HACK: COMMIT TO YOUR COLLEAGUES

Mapping is a verb. It is an intentional action. It is a collaborative process of discussing, determining, and documenting the best learning for all students.

193

Curriculum mapping, at its heart, is a documented conversation. It is meant to be a collaborative collection of ideas that represent what the actual taught curriculum is in a school. It is an ongoing process that seeks to qualify *When*, *What*, *Why*, and *How* students will learn through agreed-upon methodologies for teaching and assessment. It is a collected set of unit plans collaboratively and intentionally crafted and organized into a progression that builds knowledge bases over time. This document represents continued conversations, reflective analyses, and strategic replacements from one year to the next, and even from one unit to the next. It is a document of equity for all students.

It is also a document of collegiality and consensus. We recognize that it is a mountain to climb, but the payoff is worthwhile.

Ongoing collaboration and communication are key here. Even if an administrative directive tasks you with mapping the curriculum, don't start by filling in a bunch of boxes just to get the work done. Begin with discussion. One of the major benefits of mapping, besides improving student performance, is the transparency of learning. Talking with your colleagues, particularly those on the same grade level and content area as you, can bring illuminating ideas into the instructional program. That's good for both teachers and students. It's even better for students when they get to contribute too!

Once you start the conversation, you can decide on strategic entry points. Use the Hacks in this book for determining which standards have priority, and begin documenting your unit. Start with assessments and then unpack all the content and skills that a student would need to be proficient for the assessment. Choose a topic or theme, and align it to standards and create assessments. There is no one right way—but there are a lot of wrong ways.

Think of curriculum design in terms of what we call "Goldilocks Conditions," meaning the design is *just right*. No less and no more. It must meet the needs of both you and your students in the most efficient way possible. We still want the documentation so that we have curriculum data, but we don't need a twenty-four-volume desk set on World War II.

You may already subscribe to a particular way of documenting curriculum, or you may want to choose from one of the following processes. Make sure you pay attention to the basic design actions mentioned in the previous Hack.

- Follow a curriculum documentation protocol like Understanding by Design, where the emphasis on planning is working backward from an assessment while being considerate of overarching big ideas and transfer/learning goals.

- Consider mapping protocols that are similar to methods by Heidi Hayes Jacobs, Susan Udelhofen, Janet Hale, and Bena Kallick.

- Consider the *How*, *What*, and *Why* of the guidelines for Universal Design for Learning (UDL) through multiple means of engagement, representation, action, and expression.

- Consider a quest-based model that honors student contributions, multiple levels of questions, co-designed outcomes, different network spaces, and game design elements.

- Consider a destination-based model that promotes divergence in the *How* of learning so you can shape the *What* and *Why* along the way to the objective or assessment.

- Consider a Curriculum Cache model, a one-stop design shop that eliminates the need for daily lesson plans and records instructional actions and resources in one document that includes the traditional curricular elements, such as standards, content, skills, assessments, and vocabulary.

- Consider a model that chunks a larger unit plan into smaller sub-units that represent a series of interconnected lessons.

To avoid pitfalls, make sure you work toward a consensus with your colleagues. What can we all agree to? That agreement should be around priority standards, common assessments, even common instructional actions. The more agreement you have, the more equity you have in the system, and the easier it is to document. Many hands make light work, right?

# WHAT YOU CAN DO TOMORROW

- **Protocols for professional communication.** Your first team decision should be about how you will converse to maximize the little time you have for documenting the curriculum or curriculum mapping. Make group decisions about what the meeting is *not* for: gossip, complaints, off-topic convos, or social media distractions. It's also not a time for grading papers or doing anything other than committing to professional conversations about teaching and learning. Make group decisions about topics to discuss or document before the meeting starts so that everyone can prepare accordingly. Be sure to have all participants bring any currently documented curricular pieces with them. You may want to consider creating roles to facilitate the conversation. This could include an overall facilitator who keeps the topic on track, a timekeeper to keep the meeting moving, and/or someone in charge of a parking lot, where off-topic ideas can go for further exploration in a different meeting. An extension to this is ensuring that all voices are at the planning table. A small group of grade-level or content-area representatives sent to work on maps that everyone will use deletes opportunities for total buy-in.

- **Start with whatever you have already documented.** Teachers should already have documentation and that's your starting point. Apply what you've learned through the Hacks in this book to start refining that work, coming to consensus about what gets documented, and upgrading practices. You may want to consider applying a framework such as UbD, UDL, or any of the other documentation bullet points above.

- **Be sure you have well-defined key components of a curriculum.** At its core, a map unit must include content, skills, assessments, and the standards those three are aligned to. Consider those as non-negotiables when deciding what to document. From there, teachers will want to consider what else is worth agreeing to, and thus, worth documenting. This could include: essential questions, big ideas, transfer goals, learning targets, vocabulary, instructional actions, instructional resources, diagnostic and formative assessments, and scaffolds for student success. Be sure to be as descriptive as possible, particularly with the assessments, so that any other colleague who views your map can easily understand it.

- **Don't just create a scope and sequence.** A scope and sequence is most often the *What* and *When*—and even then, the *What* is usually distilled down to a singular idea or phrase. The document you want to create is not one of just calendaring your unit topics across the school year. A curriculum map details the *What, How,* and *How Well* (the content, the skills, and the assessments), and depending on the level of detail in the map, it may include additional elements. Adding the *When* to the curriculum map negates the need for a separate scope and sequence document. That might be marginally helpful for a quick overview of a year's worth of learning or for situating where new units or upgrades might go, but it doesn't have enough information to represent what the real, taught curriculum is, the way a curriculum map would.

- **Peer review.** Once you've completed your initial curriculum documentation, you're going to want to review it with your colleagues. Heidi Hayes Jacobs, Janet Hale, and others have written about a seven-step review process to help guide decisions about what to cut or keep or prioritize or upgrade or determine is the best way to make your map the most useful it can be. Google the phrase "Seven-Step Review Process" with the word "Mapping" to find resources related to this process.

- **Persist and reflect.** Review your maps and documentations on a regular basis. Reflect on and document what worked well, what worked OK and needs tweaking, and what didn't work. Document alternatives to what didn't work soon after you experience it to keep it fresh, and then come back to the document when you have more time and refresh it for next year with new ideas. Also, you don't have to refresh just those activities that didn't work. You can upgrade for any reason: new strategy, new technology, new interests, new connections. All this documented newness keeps your map alive and flourishing, a growing and breathing demonstration of professionalism and expertise! Use the C.L.E.A.R. Hack to help you appraise, review, and upgrade your current maps.

- **Map digitally.** Consider using a mapping system or Google Docs so that your curriculum is easily accessible to everyone. Online mapping systems give the added amenities of quick reporting and analyses, particularly when you want "at a glance" information such as a quick look at a gap analysis, overlap analysis, or standards reports. All the digital options promote continued transparency for teachers, administrators, and even parents.

## FINAL THOUGHTS

Over the years, mapping has ebbed and flowed in importance in schools. We think it is still a valuable practice for teacher teams to engage, communicate, collaborate, and come to consensus about the instructional elements in a curricular program. Systemic collegiality and conversation are essential to the health of a school and/or district. Mapping also promotes equity of instruction and removes the chance of a lottery for students, where their experiences with one teacher or another vary.

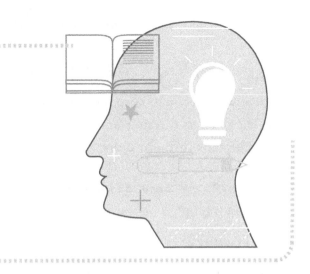

# GO C.L.E.A.R.

## Appraise your documentation to clarify curriculum

### THE PROBLEM: STATIC PLANS DON'T PROMOTE HIGHER ACHIEVEMENT

HAVE YOU TAUGHT for ten, twenty, or thirty years? Or have you taught for one year—ten, twenty, or thirty times? Static plans don't grow by themselves with contemporary times and with contemporary students. In fact, even with new standards across many content areas in the last few years, many teachers are more likely to try to salvage from previously planned lessons than recreate their curriculums. We're not saying that's bad—unless a teacher is trying to maintain what worked in 1995 so there won't be as much work to do in 2018. Unit planning and curriculum documentation is challenging work, to be sure, but it is not a one-and-done effort. We advocate for keeping a curriculum alive by actively making changes to the currently documented curriculum and being a reflective practitioner of what occurs in the classroom. To paraphrase Socrates, the unexamined practice is not worth teaching. Curriculum that doesn't change from year to year is increasingly ineffective and isn't something we want to associate with the contemporary classroom.

## THE HACK: GO C.L.E.A.R.

So, what does one do to keep the curriculum alive? We use the acronym C.L.E.A.R. when it comes to fleshing out units and connections. It asks teachers to look at their unit plans through several lenses:

- **Clarity:** When others look at your unit, do they interpret it the way you intend?

- **Liveliness**: Is the instruction lively and dynamic?

- **Evidence:** Do the assessments in your unit prove that students have mastered the skills?

- **Alignment**: Is there a balance between standards, content, skills, and assessments?

- **Robustness**: Compared to your previous unit, is this year's effort robust, hearty, and strong?

> THIS IS AN OPPORTUNITY TO BREATHE NEW LIFE INTO YOUR CURRICULUM AND INSTRUCTIONAL DESIGN, AND OFFER STUDENTS MANY REASONS TO BE INVOLVED, ATTENTIVE, AND ENGAGED.

Being C.L.E.A.R. when unit planning is essential to the big "Cs" of curriculum work: Conversation, Collaboration, and Consensus. Being C.L.E.A.R. offers opportunities for transparency, continued curriculum conversation, and natural evolution of curriculum from this point forward.

# WHAT YOU CAN DO TOMORROW

- **Start with clarity.** Share your work with your colleagues. Let them give you their take on your work. Ask them to ask you clarifying questions about what you've documented, and then listen to their ideas. If your documentation isn't clear for your colleagues, it might not be clear to your students, either.

- **You can lump liveliness and robustness together.** When you look at the ways you've taught a concept in the past, decide whether the new version is worth it. Will the instruction matter to the students? Are you creating lesson experiences (see the previous Hack) or are you creating learning roadblocks? Dated practices, old methods, ancient worksheets, and tests are all but extinct in the 21st century. How else can you make your curriculum come alive? This could be a sort of "curriculum defibrillation." This is an opportunity to breathe new life into your curriculum and instructional design, and offer students many reasons to be involved, attentive, and engaged.

- **Upgrade your evidence!** Appraising your units/maps is a good time to think about upgrading your assessments and how students will demonstrate that they've learned what you intended them to learn. Think about switching formats, switching to all constructed responses, switching to a digital presentation, or a student-created deliverable.

- **Don't skip over the alignment part.** It's probably the most important, as it informs your thinking as a practitioner about how all the parts fit together. The language of the standard(s) should inform the content and skills, with the assessments measuring those skills. The language should be similar across the plan. For instance, if a student is asked to explain something orally as a skill, but the assessment is a written task, then the written task wasn't taught or practiced. The skills could scaffold so that the oral and written are both taught and practiced, but only the written is assessed. Additionally, unit plans should have a "visual congruence" about them, too—a quick look that allows someone to perceive that the unit is mostly in alignment. Giveaways that it might not be aligned include different language between the elements, too many standards, not enough skills defined in terms of standards, essential questions and big ideas that don't seem to match at first glance, and inappropriate amounts of time for a unit based on what's included in the unit.

## FINAL THOUGHTS

Note that C.L.E.A.R. is meant to be engaged at least yearly, when teachers reflect on the previous year's practices. Appraising and reflecting on what we taught, how it was taught, the impact on student learning, and how well students demonstrated the learning are important factors in considering upgrades to the curriculum. Those upgrades applied in the coming year keep the curriculum documents fresh and ready to receive the next group of students.

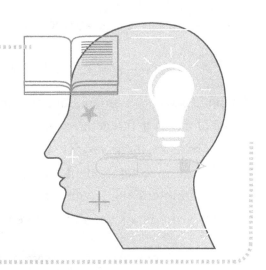

# INVITE A CURRICULUM CULTURE

See why assessment and curriculum data are equally important and cannot be separated

### THE PROBLEM: THE DATA WE ANALYZE IS RARELY A COMPLETE PICTURE OF OUR WORK

IN OUR EXPERIENCE, data meetings, if they happen, almost always focus on just assessment data. Teachers and administrators pore over the numbers and look to quantify or qualify the reason behind whether Jackie or Ajmal missed a question on the assessment—because they didn't know the information or because they were tired or because the question was no good or whatever the lens is. Sometimes they use the data to track performance over time, sometimes to improve future assessments, and sometimes as evaluation criteria for teacher effectiveness. (That, in and of itself, is a problem.)

If students are not empowered with the data results and the assessment data is not compared to the curriculum data, then teachers and their teams are lacking a fully realized curriculum culture.

## THE HACK: INVITE A CURRICULUM CULTURE

Having isolated assessment data meetings is not going to improve student performance alone. When teachers and their teams (colleagues or admins) get together to discuss assessment results, their curricula should always be in hand. They should scrutinize assessment data and curriculum data together for gaps, overlaps, and unintentional cognitive misalignments. The essential questions in these meetings should look something like this:

- When comparing our assessment data to our curriculum data, what needs to be improved, upgraded, deleted, or enhanced?

- Does the assessment data invite opportunities for reimagining instructional practice to better help students meet the demands of the assessment?

- Is the assessment the right assessment, based on our curricular goals?

- Which students need more help, and how can we make that happen?

- Was the teaching deep enough or cognitively vigorous (rigorous!) enough to meet the assessment challenges?

- How do the assessment results on this assessment compare with previous assessments, and how did that relate to the documented curriculum?

A school's curriculum culture is based on the conversations that are constant and consistent around their data—their complete sets of data—both assessment and curricular. Appraising assessment data without curricular data in hand paints a one-sided and biased version of how the assessment data is measuring student performance.

# WHAT YOU CAN DO TOMORROW

- **Bring your documented curriculum to every data meeting.**
  That's it for this action step. Just bring it with you to make it an
  invited part of every data meeting. Set a school-wide cultural goal
  for data meetings to include both assessment and curriculum data,
  and hold meeting participants responsible if any part of the data is
  missing. Be transparent!

- **Surface-level data.** When you sit down to have your meetings,
  start with assumptions. You know what you taught and how you
  taught it. Use that as a jumping-off point for generalizations about
  your expectations for student performance, including questions you
  might want to ask and predictions you might make. Those questions might include:

  - Are students doing better or worse with previously learned
    material in relation to the new material?

  - How well did everybody do in general?

  - Are there differences in question types? Which types did the
    students seem to be the most successful with?

  - Are there any patterns or trends emerging before we go
    deeper into the data?

- **Deep data dive.** The deep data dive is a more focused zone of
  analysis. We're looking for the story that the data is telling us based
  on facts only, not speculations. Questions we might ask in a deeper
  analysis include:

  - For questions that most students got incorrect, did they all
    choose the same incorrect answer?

- For similar questions, or those that were based on similar standards, were the results the same? How about when considering different question types?

- Are there any noted anomalies, such as students picking the same wrong answers or describing/writing something that is different than how they were taught?

- Were there particular questions that emerged as more difficult for everyone? Easier for everyone? How do you know?

- Based on the data, how might you sort students that are proficient from those that are not proficient? Does it come down to a handful of specific questions, or is it a more generalized pattern?

- **Develop a data ecosystem mindset.** Based on the results of your analyses, the analysts (team) should go right back to the documented curriculum for information and answers to the questions or facts that emerged. Teachers and administrators should be looking for the next best steps to enhance student learning and performance. They cannot do this with assessment data alone. The ecosystem here involves several interdependent entities: the student, the teacher, the curriculum data, and the assessment data. If any one of those things is missing, you have an incomplete ecosystem, and thus, an ecosystem in danger. Plan your action steps accordingly, and document how each of your (hopefully collaborative) decisions will impact the ecosystem elements.

## FINAL THOUGHTS

Schools that have the most impact on student learning and performance know instinctively that there are connections between performance results and curriculum data. To ignore one or the other is detrimental to the growth of the learning organization, and ultimately has a negative impact on overall student learning.

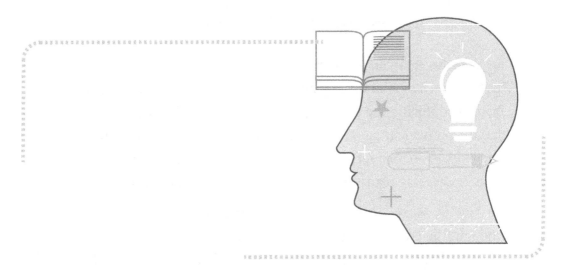

# CONCLUSION

## WHAT'S NOT HERE, AND WHY IT'S NOT HERE

**W**E'D LIKE TO address a couple of elephants as we wrap this up. Those who work with curriculum and instruction know that many elements go into a well-structured curriculum, and what we're offering here will open doors to questions about what else a teacher should add or what they can view from a different angle. We thought it would be a good idea to share with you what we didn't include so that you and your colleagues can discuss how you will attend to these additional and important decisions.

- **A specific Hack on lesson planning.** In our Hack on creating the blueprint and the Hack on lesson experiences, one of our suggestions is about skipping the granular lesson plan. While we know that many districts require teachers to write them and turn them in, we don't think the amount of time spent on them is a good return on the investment. A lot of Hacks here require the relinquishing of control, open-ended experiences, co-creation, and the addition of student voices and ideas. Granular planning doesn't play nicely with open-ended discovery and exploration. We do think that early on in a teacher's career, lesson plans have a place for documenting the pace of the lesson and the planned learning, and reflecting on what happened during the teaching moment. But once teachers have a handle on navigating a day's worth or a period's worth of learning, their time is better spent fleshing out more expansive documentation like weekly plans, units, and detailed curriculum maps.

- **A specific Hack on scope and sequence documents.** We thought the creation of a scope and sequence document is easy enough that it didn't need its own Hack. While you should definitely have a calendar-based component to your curriculum documentation, the calendar alone is only marginally helpful. Knowing when you need to teach something might offer insight into overlap in content areas or shared resources, but a scope and sequence document is limited in its usability. Instead, embed the *When* of a unit or lesson experience directly into the curriculum map.

- **Scaffolds and differentiation.** Across the breadth of this book, we cover what teachers put into place to help students achieve goals, and the multiple ways in which they can offer students choices. We've mentioned in several places that teachers may need to try different strategies based on interests and needs, and therefore didn't feel like that warranted its own Hack. To do so would have been constrictive of something that we feel should be more unfettered and organic. That's not to say that some scaffolds and differentiated choices *shouldn't* be pre-planned; if you know your students well, it makes sense that you would make instructional decisions before the teaching occurs.

- **A Hack on instructional technology.** Instructional technology has come up in several Hacks across this text in a purposeful and authentic way. There was never a time during the writing of *Hacking Instructional Design* that we planned to lead with technology. In many of the Hacks, we specifically targeted the learning objective and student choices for demonstrating their learning. Technology is meant to enhance what we're doing and perhaps make it more efficient, but it is rarely the target. As such, we don't necessarily need to hack technology so much as we need to hack the learning and connections that technology enables. Our colleague Shelly Sanchez Terrell has already done that, in her Hack Learning Book *Hacking Digital Learning Strategies*. If you want to know more about that, please check out her awesome book!

- **Learning styles and multiple intelligences.** When we were still in the classroom, we used affective surveys to discover what our students' dispositions were for learning, but we never confined them to those particular styles. There are arguments on both sides about the worth of using them, though over the years, we have seen an array of practices around them, to the betterment of, and at times detriment of, student performance. We are not necessarily convinced that grouping students in these ways pushes them. Instead, it keeps them contained in the known. That's not to say that you shouldn't allow for student voices and choices within those elements, but we would put more stock in whatever they need in the learning experience moment, rather than limiting them to labels. We don't do kids any favors when we apply any kind of learning label to them, particularly when it keeps them from exploring their own areas of interest. Labels are for adults to guide decisions, not for students to live up to or get out from under.

- **Adherence to a particular set of standards.** You'll notice that we used an array of standards throughout the text. We wanted to write and share something that was easily aligned to any standard, regardless of its source. Many states have planned obsolescence around standards anyway and will likely change or update them every few years. We wanted the ideas we shared in this book to be applicable across a wide swath of standards in any content area, and for those ideas to hold up for many years to come. With that said, we agree that if you want a systemic nature to the standards your school uses, it makes sense for the teachers to come to a consensus on the standards so there is continuity across grade levels and courses.

*Venite ad Operandum* (Let's Get to Work)

In the Spring 2018 edition of *PAPER* magazine, creative director Drew Elliott writes, "Young people don't want to accept, 'that's the way it has always been,' and guess what? They are right. Perhaps Millennials and Gen Z, deemed as the 'entitled generations,' are exactly that, entitled to equalities they were not afforded before, opportunities that were not made available and access that was once denied."

We wholeheartedly agree. Fear of losing the past is hardly a reason to slow progress. Change is coming whether we like it or not, and right now, at this moment, our power lies in *how* we embrace progress, not *whether* we embrace it. We must be careful not to design ourselves into irrelevance by failing to care about the things our students care about, or their contemporary needs. We all live in the same time, and we're not preparing for a future that is years away. We are teaching and learning for the times we live in now. If there are problems in the process—the people, the protocols, anything at all—it damages the system. If we're all in the same boat, it doesn't matter where the leak is. It matters that we are traveling—teachers and students together—boldly going into the next frontier.

Albus Dumbledore, favorite literary educator and headmaster of Hogwarts School of Witchcraft and Wizardry, once told his most famous student, "It is our choices, Harry, that show what we truly are, far more than our abilities." Truer words were never spoken. While we strongly advocate for choices for our students, we want teachers to have those choices as well.

Thus, this book is a mashup of the best books we've read, speakers we've heard, professional collaborations and conversations, and media we've experienced. These years spent reading, listening, speaking, and writing have yielded what we hope will be a useful field reference for contemporary teaching and learning. There are classical and timeless elements here, but there are also modern ones. Together, these Hacks represent a diverse range of experiences that you can choose to apply in part or in totality, depending on what you think will be most helpful to you and your students.

We'd like to end this with a *Hacking Instructional Design* Challenge.

- Be the learner you want your students to be.

- Be the teacher you wish you had.

- Never ever stop learning.

- Never ever stop inviting voices and choices into your instructional practices, whether they are from colleagues, parents, or especially students.

- Be confidently open to professional improvement and enhancement as a result of these voices.

- Always be a champion for students.

- Always be loyal to the learning and the learner.

Now, go #HackLearning.*

*Share your favorite ideas from this book using the #HackLearning hashtag. Tell us your own ideas for *Hacking Instructional Design*. Continue the conversation on Twitter and Instagram, or through our Hack Learning Facebook page. We all grow when we share!

# REFERENCES

Ainsworth, L. *Rigorous Curriculum Design: How to Create Curricular Units of Study that Align Standards, Instruction, and Assessment.* Englewood, CO: Lead Learn Press, 2010.

Airasian, P. W., et al. *Mastery Learning: Theory and Practice.* New York: Holt, Rinehart and Winston, 1971.

Alcock, M., Fisher, M., and Zmuda, A. *The Quest for Learning: How to Maximize Student Engagement.* Bloomington, IN: Solution Tree Press, 2017.

Bambrick-Santoyo, P. *Driven by Data: A Practical Guide to Improve Instruction.* Hoboken, NJ: John Wiley & Sons, 2011.

Beck, I. L., McKeown, M. G., and Kucan, L. *Bringing Words to Life: Robust Vocabulary Instruction.* New York: Guilford Press, 2013.

Buffum, A. G., Mattos, M., and Weber, C. *Pyramid Response to Intervention: RTI, Professional Learning Communities, and How to Respond When Kids Don't Learn.* Bloomington, IN: Solution Tree, 2009.

Costa, A. L. and Kallick, B. *Habits of Mind.* Alexandria, VA: Association for Supervision and Curriculum Development, 2000.

Danielson, C. *Enhancing Professional Practice: A Framework for Teaching.* Alexandria, VA: Association for Supervision and Curriculum Development, 2007.

Dewey, J. *Democracy and Education: An Introduction to the Philosophy of Education.* New York: Free Press, 1997.

Elliott, D. Dear Readers. *Paper 34*(03) (April 2018): 2.

English, F. W. and Steffy, B. E. *Curriculum Alignment: Creating a Level Playing Field for All Children on High-stakes Tests of Educational Accountability.* Lanham, MD: Scarecrow Press, 2000.

Fisher, M. *Digital Learning Strategies: How Do I Assign and Assess 21st Century Work?* Alexandria, VA: ASCD, 2013.

Glatthorn, A., et al. *Curriculum Leadership: Strategies for Development and Implementation*. Thousand Oaks, CA: SAGE Publications, 2016.

Hale, J. A. and Dunlap, R. F. *An Educational Leader's Guide to Curriculum Mapping: Creating and Sustaining Collaborative Cultures*. Thousand Oaks, CA: Corwin, 2010.

Hale, J. A. and Fisher, M. *Upgrade Your Curriculum: Practical Ways to Transform Units and Engage Students*. Alexandria, VA: ASCD, 2013.

Hargreaves, A. and Fullan, M. *Professional Capital: Transforming Teaching in Every School*. New York: Teachers College Press, 2012.

Heath, C. and Heath, D. *Switch: How to Change Things When Change Is Hard*. London: Random House Business, 2011.

Jacobs, H. H. *Curriculum 21: Essential Education for a Changing World*. Alexandria, VA: ASCD, 2010.

Jacobs, H. H. *Getting Results With Curriculum Mapping*. Alexandria, VA: Association for Supervision and Curriculum Development, 2004.

Jacobs, H. H. *Active Literacy Across the Curriculum: Connecting Print Literacy With Digital, Media, and Global Competence, K–12*. New York: Routledge, 2018.

Kallick, B. and Colosimo, J. *Using Curriculum Mapping and Assessment Data to Improve Learning*. Thousand Oaks, CA: Corwin Press, 2009.

Kallick, B. and Zmuda, A. *Students at the Center: Personalized Learning With Habits of Mind*. Alexandria, VA: ASCD, 2017.

Kim, K. H., Ph.D. (2011, November 09). The Creativity Crisis: The Decrease in Creative Thinking Scores on the Torrance Tests of Creative Thinking. https://www.tandfonline.com/doi/abs/10.1080/10400419.2011.627805 (accessed March 17, 2018).

Lesaux, N. K., Galloway, E. P., and Marietta, S. H. *Teaching Advanced Literacy Skills: A Guide for Leaders in Linguistically Diverse Schools*. New York: Guilford Press, 2016.

# REFERENCES

Marzano, R. J., Pickering, D. J., and Pollock, J. E. *Classroom Instruction That Works: Research-based Strategies for Increasing Student Achievement.* Alexandria, VA: Association for Supervision and Curriculum Development, 2008.

Parnes, S. and Osborn, A. (n.d.). The CPS Process. http://www.creativeeducationfoundation.org/creative-problem-solving/the-cps-process/ (accessed February 5, 2018).

Pinar, W. F., et al. *Understanding Curriculum: An Introduction to the Study of Historical and Contemporary Curriculum Discourses.* New York: Lang, 2014.

Pinnell, G. S. and Fountas, I. C. *The Continuum of Literacy Learning, Grades PreK–8: A Guide to Teaching.* Portsmouth, NH: Heinemann, 2011.

Purkey, W. W. and Novak, J. M. *Inviting School Success: A Self-concept Approach to Teaching, Learning, and Democratic Practice.* Belmont, CA: Wadsworth Pub, 1996.

Robinson, K. (n.d.). Do schools kill creativity? https://www.ted.com/talks/ken_robinson_says_schools_kill_creativity (accessed February 2, 2018).

Rowling, J. K. *Harry Potter and the Order of the Phoenix.* New York: Scholastic, 2004.

Sackstein, S. *Hacking Assessment: 10 Ways to Go Gradeless in a Traditional Grades School.* Cleveland: Times 10 Publications, 2015.

Schell, J. *The Art of Game Design: A Book of Lenses.* Amsterdam: Elsevier, 2010.

Sprenger, M. *Vocab Rehab: How Do I Teach Vocabulary Effectively in a Limited Time?* Alexandria, VA: ASCD, 2014.

Terrell, S. S. *Hacking Digital Learning Strategies: 10 Ways to Launch Edtech Missions in Your Classroom.* Cleveland: Times 10 Publications, 2017.

Tolisano, S. R. and Hale, J. A. *A Guide to Documenting Learning: Making Thinking Visible, Meaningful, Shareable, and Amplified.* Thousand Oaks, CA: Corwin, a Sage Publishing Company, 2018.

Torrance, E. P. and Safter, H. T. *The Incubation Model of Teaching: Getting Beyond the Aha!* Buffalo: Bearly, 1990.

Tyler, R. W. *Basic Principles of Curriculum and Instruction*. Chicago: The University of Chicago Press, 2013.

Udelhofen, S. *Keys to Curriculum Mapping: Strategies and Tools to Make It Work*. Thousand Oaks, CA: Corwin Press, 2005.

Wagner, T. *The Global Achievement Gap: Why Even Our Best Schools Don't Teach the New Survival Skills Our Children Need—and What We Can Do About It*. New York: Basic Books, 2014.

Westby, E. L. and Dawson, V. L. "Creativity: Asset or Burden in the Classroom?" *Creativity Research Journal* 8:1, 1-10 (2010), https://www.tandfonline.com/doi/abs/10.1207/s15326934crj0801_1.

Wiggins, G. P. and McTighe, J. *Understanding by Design*. Alexandria, VA: Association for Supervision and Curriculum Development, 2008.

Zmuda, A. and Thompson, J. *How to Leverage Personalized Learning in the Classroom* eBook. March 2018. https://info.freshgrade.com/personalized-learning-ebook (accessed April 5, 2018).

Zmuda, A., Ullman, D., and Curtis, G. *Learning Personalized: The Evolution of the Contemporary Classroom*. San Francisco: Jossey-Bass, 2015.

# A NOTE ON CITATIONS

**E**ACH OF THE Hacks in *Hacking Instructional Design* follows a problem/solution/action formula so the reader can easily identify elements of the Hack that will be most meaningful for them. It's analogous to a tool like Pinterest, where one can find unique and more efficient ways to tackle interesting projects. Even with its formulaic approach, this is not a "theory into practice" book. This is a book about best practices that are intended to help teachers gain insight and ideas from what we've shared. That said, it's more of a *practice informs better practice* book. As such, in-text citations that would support theoretical evidence are not included in the traditional way. As professional developers, we often weave several theoretical frameworks together for maximum impact when we work with schools. The same is true here. We married ideas from a huge cadre of curriculum and educational experts, including Larry Ainsworth, Marie Alcock, Floyd Boschee, Bonni Boschee, Art Costa, Greg Curtis, Fenwick English, Michael Fullan, Allan Glatthorn, Janet Hale, Andy Hargreaves, Chip Heath, Dan Heath, Heidi Hayes Jacobs, Bena Kallick, Robert Marzano, Jay McTighe, William Pinar, William Purkey, William Reynolds, Patrick Slattery, Peter Taubman, Jill Thompson, Silvia Rosenthal Tolisano, Ralph Tyler, Susan Udelhofen, Diane Ullman, Tony Wagner, Bruce Whitehead, Grant Wiggins, and Allison Zmuda.

These ideas, along with our own, and informed by more than two decades of work in schools, bring us to this moment of integrated practices. Our professional decisions are guided by our predecessors, and where we shared something specific to a framework, idea, or person, we wrote into the narrative who those educational experts are and where (or how) their collective ideas informed our practices around these Hacks. Additionally, we have included a bibliographic reference section. It is our sincere hope that you will extend your own professional learning by further investigating the ideas by these important educators and thought leaders.

—MICHAEL AND ELIZABETH FISHER

## HACKING EDUCATION
### 10 Quick Fixes For Every School
*By Mark Barnes (@markbarnes19) & Jennifer Gonzalez (@cultofpedagogy)*

In the award-winning first Hack Learning Series book, *Hacking Education*, Mark Barnes and Jennifer Gonzalez employ decades of teaching experience and hundreds of discussions with education thought leaders to show you how to find and hone the quick fixes that every school and classroom need. Using a Hacker's mentality, they provide **one Aha moment after another** with 10 Quick Fixes For Every School—solutions to everyday problems and teaching methods that any teacher or administrator can implement immediately.

"Barnes and Gonzalez don't just solve problems; they turn teachers into hackers—a transformation that is right on time."

—Don Wettrick, Author of *Pure Genius*

## HACKING PROJECT BASED LEARNING
### 10 Easy Steps to PBL and Inquiry in the Classroom

*By Ross Cooper (@rosscoops31) and Erin Murphy (@murphysmusings5)*

As questions and mysteries around PBL and inquiry continue to swirl, experienced classroom teachers and school administrators Ross Cooper and Erin Murphy have written a book that will empower those intimidated by PBL to cry, "I can do this!" while at the same time providing added value for those who are already familiar with the process.

Impacting teachers and leaders around the world, *Hacking Project Based Learning* demystifies what PBL is all about with **10 hacks that construct a simple path** that educators and students can easily follow to achieve success. Forget your prior struggles with project based learning. This book makes PBL an amazing gift you can give all students tomorrow!

"*Hacking Project Based Learning* is a classroom essential. Its ten simple 'hacks' will guide you through the process of setting up a learning environment in which students will thrive from start to finish."

—DANIEL H. PINK, NEW YORK TIMES BESTSELLING AUTHOR OF *DRIVE*

## HACKING ASSESSMENT
### 10 Ways To Go Gradeless In a Traditional Grades School

*By Starr Sackstein (@mssackstein)*

In the bestselling *Hacking Assessment*, award-winning teacher and world-renowned formative assessment expert Starr Sackstein unravels one of education's oldest mysteries: How to assess learning without grades—even in a school that uses numbers, letters, GPAs, and report cards. While many educators can only muse about the possibility of a world without grades, teachers like Sackstein are **reimagining education.** In this unique, eagerly-anticipated book, Sackstein shows you exactly how to create a remarkable no-grades classroom like hers, a vibrant place where students grow, share, thrive, and become independent learners who never ask, "What's this worth?"

"The beauty of the book is that it is not an empty argument against grades—but rather filled with valuable alternatives that are practical and will help to refocus the classroom on what matters most."

—ADAM BELLOW, WHITE HOUSE PRESIDENTIAL INNOVATION FELLOW

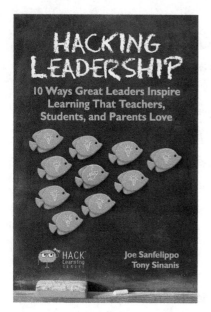

## HACKING LEADERSHIP
### 10 Ways Great Leaders Inspire Learning That Teachers, Students, and Parents Love

*By Joe Sanfelippo (@joe_sanfelippo) and Tony Sinanis (@tonysinanis)*

In the runaway bestseller *Hacking Leadership*, internationally known school leaders Joe Sanfelippo and Tony Sinanis bring readers inside schools that few stakeholders have ever seen—places where students not only come first but have a unique voice in teaching and learning. Sanfelippo and Sinanis ignore the bureaucracy that stifles many leaders, focusing instead on building a culture of **engagement, transparency and, most important, fun**. *Hacking Leadership* has superintendents, principals, and teacher leaders around the world employing strategies they never before believed possible and learning how to lead from the middle. Want to revolutionize teaching and learning at your school or district? *Hacking Leadership* is your blueprint. Read it today; energize teachers and learners tomorrow!

"The authors do a beautiful job of helping leaders focus inward, instead of outward. This is an essential read for leaders who are, or want to lead, learner-centered schools."

—GEORGE COUROS, AUTHOR OF *THE INNOVATOR'S MINDSET*

## HACKING SCHOOL CULTURE
### Designing Compassionate Classrooms

*By Angela Stockman (@angelastockman) and Ellen Feig Gray (@ellenfeiggray)*

Bullying prevention and character-building programs are deepening our awareness of how today's kids struggle and how we might help, but many agree: They aren't enough to create school cultures where students and staff flourish. This inspired Angela Stockman and Ellen Feig Gray to begin seeking out systems and educators who were getting things right. Their experiences taught them that the **real game changers are using a human-centered approach**. Inspired by other design thinkers, many teachers are creating learning environments where seeking a greater understanding of themselves and others is the highest standard. They're also realizing that compassion is best cultivated in the classroom, not the boardroom or the auditorium. It's here that we learn how to pull one another close. It's here that we begin to negotiate the distances between us, too.

"*Hacking School Culture: Designing Compassionate Classrooms* is a valuable addition to the Hack Learning Series. It provides concrete support and suggestions for teachers to improve their interactions with their students at the same time they enrich their own professional experiences. Although primarily aimed at K–12 classrooms, the authors' insightful suggestions have given me, a veteran college professor, new insights into positive classroom dynamics which I have already begun to incorporate into my classes."

—LOUISE HAINLINE, PH.D., PROFESSOR OF PSYCHOLOGY,
BROOKLYN COLLEGE OF CUNY

## HACKING EARLY LEARNING
### 10 Building Blocks to Success in Pre-K–3 That All Teachers and School Leaders Should Know

*By Jessica Cabeen (@jessicacabeen)*

School readiness, closing achievement gaps, partnering with families, and innovative learning are just a few of the reasons the early learning years are the most critical years in a child's life. In what ways have schools lost the critical components of early learning—preschool through third grade—and how can we intentionally bring those ideas and instructional strategies back? In *Hacking Early Learning*, kindergarten school leader, early childhood education specialist, and Minnesota State Principal of the Year Jessica Cabeen provides strategies for teachers, principals, and district administrators for **best practices in preschool through third grade,** including connecting these strategies to all grade levels.

"Jessica Cabeen is not afraid to say she's learned from her mistakes and misconceptions. But it is those mistakes and misconceptions that qualify her to write this book, with its wonderfully user-friendly format. For each problem specified, there is a hack and actionable advice presented as "What You Can Do Tomorrow" and "A Blueprint for Full Implementation." Jessica's leadership is informed by both head and heart and, because of that, her wisdom will be of value to those who wish to teach and lead in the early childhood field."

—RAE PICA, EARLY CHILDHOOD EDUCATION KEYNOTE SPEAKER AND AUTHOR OF *WHAT IF EVERYBODY UNDERSTOOD CHILD DEVELOPMENT?*

## HACKING ENGAGEMENT
### 50 Tips & Tools to Engage Teachers and Learners Daily

*By James Alan Sturtevant (@jamessturtevant)*

Some students hate your class. Others are just bored. Many are too nice, or too afraid, to say anything about it. Don't let it bother you; it happens to the best of us. But now, it's **time to engage!** In *Hacking Engagement*, the seventh book in the Hack Learning Series, veteran high school teacher, author, and popular podcaster James Sturtevant provides 50—that's right five-oh—tips and tools that will engage even the most reluctant learners daily. Sold in dozens of countries around the world, *Hacking Engagement* has become an educator's go-to guide for better student engagement in all grades and subjects. In fact, this book is so popular, Sturtevant penned a follow-up, *Hacking Engagement Again*, which brings 50 more powerful strategies. Find both at HackLearningBooks.com.

## HACKING DIGITAL LEARNING STRATEGIES
### 10 Ways to Launch EdTech Missions in Your Classroom

*By Shelly Sanchez Terrell (@ShellTerrell)*

In this breakthrough book, international EdTech presenter and NAPW Woman of the Year Shelly Sanchez Terrell demonstrates the power of EdTech Missions—lessons and projects that inspire learners to use web tools and social media to innovate, research, collaborate, problem-solve, campaign, crowd fund, crowdsource, and publish. The 10 Missions in *Hacking DLS* are more than enough to transform how teachers integrate technology, but there's also much more here. Included in the book is a **38-page Mission Toolkit**, complete with reproducible mission cards, badges, polls, and other handouts that you can copy and distribute to students immediately.

"The secret to Shelly's success as an education collaborator on a global scale is that she shares information most revered by all educators, information that is original, relevant, and vetted, combining technology with proven education methodology in the classroom. This book provides relevance to a 21st-century educator."

—THOMAS WHITBY, AUTHOR, PODCASTER, BLOGGER, CONSULTANT, CO-FOUNDER OF #EDCHAT

## HACKING CLASSROOM MANAGEMENT
### 10 Ideas To Help You Become the Type of Teacher They Make Movies About
*By Mike Roberts (@baldroberts)*

Utah English Teacher of the Year and sought-after speaker Mike Roberts brings you 10 quick and easy classroom management hacks that will **make your classroom the place to be** for all your students. He shows you how to create an amazing learning environment that actually makes discipline, rules, and consequences obsolete, no matter if you're a new teacher or a 30-year veteran teacher.

"Mike writes from experience; he's learned, sometimes the hard way, what works and what doesn't, and he shares those lessons in this fine little book. The book is loaded with specific, easy-to-apply suggestions that will help any teacher create and maintain a classroom where students treat one another with respect, and where they learn."

—CHRIS CROWE, ENGLISH PROFESSOR AT BYU, PAST PRESIDENT OF ALAN, AUTHOR OF *DEATH COMING UP THE HILL, GETTING AWAY WITH MURDER: THE TRUE STORY OF THE EMMETT TILL CASE; MISSISSIPPI TRIAL, 1955*

## HACKING THE WRITING WORKSHOP
### Redesign with Making in Mind

*By Angela Stockman (@AngelaStockman)*

Agility matters. This is what Angela Stockman learned when she left the classroom over a decade ago to begin supporting young writers and their teachers in schools. What she learned transformed her practice and led to the publication of her primer on this topic: *Make Writing: 5 Teaching Strategies that Turn Writer's Workshop Into a Maker Space.* Now, Angela is back with more stories from the road and **plenty of new thinking** to share. In *Make Writing*, Stockman upended the traditional writing workshop by combining it with the popular ideas that drive the maker space. Now, she is expanding her concepts and strategies and breaking new ground in *Hacking the Writing Workshop*.

"Good writing is good thinking. This is a book about how to think better, for yourself and with others."

—DAVE GRAY, FOUNDER OF XPLANE, AND AUTHOR OF *THE CONNECTED COMPANY*, *GAMESTORMING*, AND *LIMINAL THINKING*

## THE UNSERIES Teaching Reimagined

The uNseries is for teachers who love the uNlovable, accept the uNacceptable, rebuild the broken, and help the genius soar. Through each book in the uNseries, you will learn how to continue your growth as a teacher, leader, and influencer. The goal is that together we can become better than we ever could be alone. Each chapter uNveils an important principle to ponder, uNravels a plan that you can put into place to make an even greater impact, and uNleashes an action step for you to take to be a better educator. Learn more about the **uNseries and everything uN** at unseries.com.

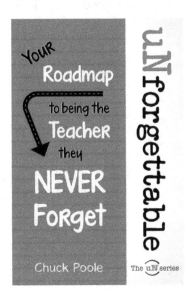

### uNforgettable
**Your Roadmap to Being the Teacher They Never Forget**

*by Chuck Poole (@cpoole27)*

"These 10 destinations will give you the inspiration and knowledge you need to take action and leave a lasting impression for years to come. Chuck Poole will be your guide. Through every twist and turn, you will be empowered, encouraged, and equipped to reimagine teaching in a way that will influence your students for a lifetime."

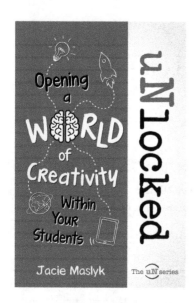

## uNlocked:
### Opening a World of Creativity Within Your Students

*By Jacie Maslyk (@DrJacieMaslyk)*

Creativity flows within us all. It allows teachers to reignite a passion for learning and offers students an outlet that can lead to endless possibilities. Creativity is essential, and Jacie Maslyk helps you and your students uNleash its full potential with her new book, *uNlocked: Opening a World of Creativity Within Your Students.*

In this second book in The uNseries, you will learn how to **uNlock creativity in powerful ways** to help you create undeniable learning experiences for your students, and you will discover the keys you need to uNlock your students' full potential for creativity.

# HACK LEARNING RESOURCES

## SITES:
times10books.com
hacklearning.org
hacklearningbooks.com
unseries.com
teachonomy.com

## PODCASTS:
hacklearningpodcast.com
jamesalansturtevant.com/podcast
teachonomy.com/podcast

## FREE TOOLKIT FOR TEACHERS:
hacklearningtoolkit.com

## ON TWITTER:
@HackMyLearning
#HackLearning
#HackLearningDaily
#WeTeachuN
#HackingLeadership
#HackingMath
#HackingLiteracy
#HackingEngagement
#HackingHomework

#HackingPBL
#MakeWriting
#EdTechMissions
#MovieTeacher
#HackingEarlyLearning
#CompassionateClassrooms
#HackGoogleEdu
#HackYourLibrary
#QuitPoint

## HACK LEARNING ON FACEBOOK:
facebook.com/hacklearningseries

## HACK LEARNING ON INSTAGRAM:
hackmylearning

# ABOUT THE AUTHORS

**Michael Fisher** is an author, instructional coach, and educational consultant specializing in the intersection between instructional technology and curriculum design. He works with districts in the United States and Canada to help teachers and schools maximize available technology, software, and web-based resources while attending to curriculum design, instructional practices, and assessments. This is his second book in the Hack Learning Series, following 2016's *Hacking the Common Core*. You can contact him via Twitter @fisher1000 or by visiting his website at www.digigogy.com.

**Elizabeth Fisher** is an instructional coach and educational consultant specializing in literacy, English Language Arts, and curriculum design. She works with teachers and administrators across Western New York to help them improve their professional practices. You can contact her via Twitter @elizabethfisher.

Together, Michael and Elizabeth have been educating students and teachers for more than two decades. This is their first full-length book together, following co-created journal articles and professional development around parent involvement, brain-based learning, and differentiated instruction. They have two children, Lily and Charlotte, members of both Generations Z and Alpha, respectively, who keep them on their toes.

# ACKNOWLEDGMENTS

**A**s is always the case, good work is never done in isolation. We are so grateful for the cadre of people who have been willing to give their time, expertise, and feedback to help improve upon our ideas, including Matthew Zayas, Crista Anderson, and Sheila Murphy.

We are especially grateful to Andrew Krazmien, Johni Cruse Craig, Ed.D., Keith Mason, and Craig Gastauer for their very thoughtful and insightful feedback. We appreciate that you interacted with us and with other feedback providers to help us be more precise about our message.

We would like to thank Chevin Stone, M.Ed., and Bryn Coape-Arnold, both Hack Learning Ambassadors. We appreciate your willingness to read and respond so quickly. You are valued members of the Hack Learning community and we are grateful for your feedback.

For many years, we have benefitted from the expertise, ideas, and camaraderie of our sisters, Janet Hale and Allison Zmuda. We value their opinions and feedback, and their willingness to always make what we do better. Thank you again for your in-depth responses and conversations about this work.

We would like to thank all of the incredible educators listed in the bibliography section. What we have created here is a compendium of knowledge that has been influenced by many. Thank you for sharing your ideas with the world. They have certainly impacted us and, by extension, will continue to have an impact for many years to come.

And finally, we would like to thank Mark Barnes for having this vision of Hacking Learning and improving education with practical strategies for every educator. We appreciate being invited into this action-oriented educational ecosystem.

# X10

## Vision, Experience, Action

**Times 10** is helping all education stakeholders improve every aspect of teaching and learning. We are committed to solving big problems with simple ideas. We bring you content from experts, shared through multiple channels, including books, podcasts, and an array of social networks. Our mantra is simple: Read it today; fix it tomorrow. Stay in touch with us at Times10Books.com, at #HackLearning on Twitter, and on the Hack Learning Facebook page.

CPSIA information can be obtained
at www.ICGtesting.com
Printed in the USA
LVHW020254200722
723870LV00007B/369